Inge Ostepho

CW01313913

ABIDING

To Inge + Bill,
May this book minister to your heart and strengthen your relationship with Jesus.
with love,
Maria

ABIDING
THE JOY OF OUR SALVATION

MARIA KELLY

Xulon Press

Copyright © 2017 by Maria Kelly

Abiding
The JOY Of Our Salvation
by Maria Kelly

Printed in the United States of America.

ISBN 9781545603178

All rights reserved solely by the author. The author guarantees all contents are original and do not infringe upon the legal rights of any other person or work. No part of this book may be reproduced in any form without the permission of the author. The views expressed in this book are not necessarily those of the publisher.

Unless otherwise indicated, Scripture quotations taken from the Holy Bible, New International Version (NIV). Copyright © 1973, 1978, 1984, 2011 by Biblica, Inc.™. Used by permission. All rights reserved.

Scripture quotations taken from the New American Standard Bible (NASB). Copyright © 1960, 1962, 1963, 1968, 1971, 1972, 1973, 1975, 1977, 1995 by The Lockman Foundation. Used by permission. All rights reserved.

Scripture quotations taken from the Holy Bible, New International Version (NIV). Copyright © 1973, 1978, 1984, 2011 by Biblica, Inc.™. Used by permission. All rights reserved.

cripture quotations taken from the New King James Version (NKJV). Copyright © 1982 by Thomas Nelson, Inc. Used by permission. All rights reserved.

Scripture quotations taken from the New Testament in Modern English by J.B Philips (PHILLIPS). Copyright © 1960, 1972 J. B. Phillips. Administered by The Archbishops' Council of the Church of England. Used by Permission.

www.xulonpress.com

TABLE OF CONTENTS

Acknowledgment xi

Introduction. xiii

1. Are You Experiencing the Joy of Your Salvation? 1
    Jesus' Promise in John 14:1-4,23b

2. Do You Struggle to Feel God's Presence? 10
    What We Experience When We Suffer

3. Jesus: the Way, Truth, and Life 18
    John 14:4-9
    Do I Look to Jesus as the Author and Perfecter of My Life?

4. How Do We Take Hold of the Peace and Rest of Christ? 24
    John 14:27
    Are My Eyes on Jesus or on Idols?

5. The Joy of the Word 36
    John 1:1-14
    Distracted by Many Things
    Hearing Him through the "Parable of the Sower
    and the Soil"

6. Do You Believe Jesus is Actually Living in You?. 52
    The Promise of the Holy Spirit: John 14:15-26

7. Do We Imitate or Integrate the Life of Christ? 62
    A Demonstration Symbolizing Baptism in Christ

8. Understanding the Abiding Life 76
    John 15:1-17

9. How the Fruit of the Spirit is Produced in our Lives 84
    John 15:18-21
    What are the Gifts of the Spirit and How do We
    Receive Them?

10. If I Have The Joy Of God's Salvation, Should I
    Experience Grief and Sorrow, ... 95
    James 1:2-4; John 15:18-21
    John 15:18-21; 16:20, 33

TABLE OF CONTENTS

    Lamentations, Crying Out To God, Grief, And Despair in Scripture?

11. If We Abide in Christ, are We to be Fearful? 109
    John 15:18-21

12. "What a Privilege to Carry Everything to God in Prayer" 119
    An Unexpected Example of Joy in Prayer—January 16th
    When I Cannot Carry My Needs to God in Prayer

13. Forgiveness, the Key to the Kingdom of Heaven, Abiding Joy, and Peace 126
    Matthew 16:13-19; John 20:21-23
    Forgiveness—What it is And What it is Not

14. I Just Want to Be Where You Are 138

Notes 143

ACKNOWLEDGMENT

My appreciation and gratitude go to many who have been an encouragement and blessing in my life. Foremost, my husband, Bill, of forty-seven years, the many pastors who have faithfully served as my teachers, as well as all my small group Bible study teachers. In addition, a huge affectionate hug to my faithful sisters in Christ who were so open and receptive to my teaching on the abiding life in Christ, and lastly, those who diligently read and critiqued this book — Pat Fros, Lee Anderson, and Cheryl Rhoads. Last but not least, my eternal praise and thanksgiving goes to my Lord and Savior, Jesus, my heavenly Abba, and His Spirit in whom I live and move and have my being.

INTRODUCTION

Many years ago, I felt God spoke and told me He would have me write a book. I shared this with my husband, so for years he would ask when I would write this book. My answer always was, "When God tells me to and leads me to write about a topic of His choosing." So this appears to be the time and the topic of His choosing.

I also knew that whenever God moved me to write, I would experience it in a similar way that the Apostle Paul expressed in I Corinthians 9:16: *"When I preach the gospel, I cannot boast, for I am compelled to preach. Woe to me if I do not preach the gospel."* So, even though I have been resisting, I feel I can no longer disobey God's compelling call and believe (by faith) that I am to write this book.

Since I have never written a book, I felt a lot of anxiety and self-doubt. I questioned God, "Why me and why would, what I write, have any credibility, since I am an unknown? Haven't there been many books written about our relationship in Christ?" His answer to me was, "Like Abraham you have to do this in obedience by faith. I will lead you." I knew I had heard my heavenly Father, yet I needed a lot of assurance. These are some of the Scriptures He brought to mind to assure me I was hearing His voice. Jesus, The Good Shepherd, told us, *"My sheep hear my voice, and I know them, and they follow me" (John 10:27, NAS)*. *"'Righteous Father, though the world has not known you, I known you;... I have made you known to them, and will continue to make you known in order that the love you have for me may be in them and that I myself my be in them'"* (John 17:25–26). The Apostle Paul wrote these words in I Corinthians 2:7–16: *"We speak of God's secret a wisdom that has been hidden,... but God revealed it to us by his Spirit;...* **we have the mind of Christ***"* (emphasis added).

From these verses, it is clear that if we have God's Spirit, we can hear His voice and know His mind. I'm sure that most of you have heard His voice. Each of us may experience hearing Him in a uniquely different way, but this is how I hear Him speak—it is not an audible voice but the still, sense that comes as a flow of thoughts. As I receive these thoughts, my spirit recognizes them as His voice, and there is a peace and joy that resonates deep within, which can only be attributed or understood through the experience of faith. It is as described in the above passage in I Corinthians 2.

I believe all of us have times when we question whether we are hearing from God. At those times, all we can do is to continue in prayer before Him and then step out in faith. We are told in Hebrews 11:1 that *"Now faith is being sure of what we hope for and certain of what we do not see."* Confirmation comes in several possible ways: the Spirit in a brother or sister in Christ bears witness to my Spirit,

INTRODUCTION

what has been said and done bears fruit in the lives to whom you are ministering, and having a deep sense of peace, and joy.

In addition, it is always affirming to read words of Christian authors, who have a strong walk with Jesus. One such author is Oswald Chambers, whose writing has ministered to my heart for many years. This is what he writes about hearing God's voice, struggling with questions of whether you are hearing correctly, and obeying: "

> Just because I don't understand what Jesus Christ says, I have no right to determine that He must be mistaken in what He says... I know when the instructions have come from God because of their quiet persistence. But when I begin to weigh the *pros* and *cons,* and doubt and debate enter into my mind, I am bringing in an element that is not of God. This will only result in my concluding that His instructions to me were not right... Faithfulness to Jesus means that I must step out even when and where I can't see anything (see *Matthew 14:29*)... Faith, however, is not intellectual understanding; faith is a deliberate commitment to the Person of Jesus Christ, even when I can't see the way ahead.

Are you debating whether you should take a step of faith in Jesus, or whether you should wait until you

> can clearly see how to do what He has asked? Simply obey Him with unrestrained joy... Are you faithful to what He says, or are you trying to compromise His words with thoughts that never came from Him? "Whatever He says to you, *do it*" (John 2:5)."[1]

Recently, I watched an old movie titled *The Song of Bernadette*, which is about a young girl who unexpectedly is given a sign from God and spoken to by Jesus' mother Mary. No one, including the local priest, initially believed her and so she was persecuted and called crazy. But later as she persevered and the miraculous signs bore witness to her words, the priest said this: "For those who believe, no explanation is required, but for those who don't believe, no explanation is possible." Like Bernadette, I can't explain the why. All I can do is to walk in obedience to Jesus and bring joy to His heart. In no way am I claiming to know all there is to know about God, His salvation, or the *abiding life*. He is too vast, and I am conscious of the words written in Isaiah 55:8–9: *"For my thoughts are not your thoughts, neither are your ways my ways, as the heavens are higher than the earth, so are my ways higher than your ways and my thoughts than your thoughts."*

There are several reasons I am taking so much time in writing this introduction: first, because, to some people, talking to God is seen as a mental illness, so I have to continually go back to Him for His assurance. Second, most of this book is based upon the truths I have received from Jesus in my intimate conversations with Him. Over the years, although I have learned to recognize and listen to His voice, be led by Him, hear His heart and mind, and place my confidence in Him, there is always room to question whether one is truly hearing from God or if the thoughts are just one's own. I feel very unworthy and humbled and—yes even fearful—as I step out in faith to write.

I am writing as my husband and I are taking a winter retreat from the long, cold, drab Michigan winters. When we first planned the getaway, I debated with my husband about the length of time, since I felt two months was too long a time away from ministry commitments and family. However, he insisted. As I was praying—or should I say, debating with—God about the length of time, He helped me to see that He was once again leading me through my husband, and the time was needed because He was going to have me write the long-awaited book.

Once I had heard this, I had a peace about the length of time; however, my mind was quickly filled with questions about the topic. At first, I had a deep sense of sadness (grief), and felt He was sad that so many of His children struggle to please Him and have little to no joy in their life with Christ. Then these words came to me; **"Restore to me the joy of your salvation"** (Psalm 51:12a, emphasis added). I felt that deep sense of peace of which I spoke earlier—that this was God's voice and that this was to be the focus of the book. In addition, I felt that He wanted me to share the truths He had been teaching me on "the abiding Life." So, the title was born: *Abiding: The Joy of Our Salvation*.

ABIDING

When we first arrived in Texas I spent several days walking on the beach, resisting, and questioning Father about doing this. As the first few days past, I became increasingly restless, but God patiently gave me verses, readings, and loved one's words (unbeknownst to them) to urge me to start writing. I had not spoken to anyone about this, not even my husband. It felt overwhelming, like standing at the bottom of a mountain and looking up, knowing I had to get to the top but having no idea how. So, even though I felt overwhelmed, I chose to follow in obedience and love for my heavenly Father, Jesus, and you my brothers and sister in Christ.

And so I begin with this prayer for myself from Psalm 51:10–12: *"Create in me a pure heart, O God, and renew a steadfast spirit within me…. Restore to me the joy of your salvation, and grant me with a willing spirit…"*

This is my prayer for you, as you read this book:

> *"I keep asking that the God our Lord Jesus Christ, the glorious Father, may give you the Spirit of wisdom and revelation, so that you may know him better. I pray also that the eyes of your heart may be enlightened in order that you may know the hope to which he has called you, the riches of his glorious inheritance in the saints, and his incomparably great power for us who believe."* (Eph. 1:17–19).

CHAPTER 1
ARE YOU EXPERIENCING THE JOY OF YOUR SALVATION?

Jesus' Promise in John 14:1-4, 23b

The Scriptures are filled with God's promises, that we will have joy and that He rejoices when we are in relationship with Him. Here are just a few:

Luke 15:6–7, 9–10, Jesus speaking*: "'Rejoice with me; I have found my lost sheep. I tell you that in the same way there will be more rejoicing in heaven over one sinner who repents than over ninety-nine righteous persons who do not need to repent; Rejoice with me; I have found my lost coin.' In the same way, I tell you, there is rejoicing in the presence of the angels of God…"* The lost can be interpreted both as the unsaved (lost), who are then saved (found), as well as those of us who have lost the way and fallen into sin (lost) and now have repented (found).

Luke 10:20b— *"'rejoice that your names are written in heaven.'" Psalm 21:6 says, "Surely you have granted him eternal blessings and made him glad with the joy of your presence."*

Psalm 89:15–16: *"Blessed are those who have learned to acclaim you, who walk in the light of your presence, O LORD, they rejoice in your name all day long."*

Acts 2:28: *"You have made known to me the paths of life; you will fill me with joy in your presence."*

John 15:9–11: *"As the Father has loved me, so have I loved you. Now remain (abide) in my love.... I have told you this so that my joy may be in you and that your joy may be complete."*

I Peter 1:8: *"Though you have not seen him, you love him; and even though you do not see him now, you believe in him and are filled with an inexpressible and glorious joy,..."*

As you may have noticed in the verses above, joy is in direct connection to being with Him in His Kingdom—in His presence. So the question becomes, why do so many of us, His children, lack joy or struggle to experience this joy? This was also my struggle for most of my thirty years of Christianity, and this may be yours too and the reason you picked up this book. Let's make the question more personal. Do you struggle to feel God's presence, and if you do, do you question why? And do you wish you could experience more peace and joy in your Christian walk? You are not alone.

It is important before we delve into answering these questions to clarify the difference between joy and happiness—a state we often pursue as our "American right." The word happiness is not found in Scripture; however the words "joy" and "blessed" are. Joy in Greek and Hebrew means: "cheerfulness, i.e. calm delight: — gladness, joy (full, fullness); be well; graciousness of manner, of act; (lit., fig. or spiritual): espec. **The divine influence upon the heart, and its reflection in the life**,(emphasis added) including gratitude; acceptable, benefit, favour, gift, grace (-ous), pleasure." It is of note, that the word "happiness" is NOT part of the definition, and that joy is a "divine gift."

Now let's return to the earlier questions of why we may not experience joy. There can be many reasons, but I will try to focus on some of the possible reasons. God has shown me that one of these reasons may be that we misunderstand John 14:1–3. Many of us, which included me for many years, have interpreted this Scripture as a promise by Jesus to His disciples of Heaven and eternal life with Him after we die and/or His second coming. Often we hear this Scripture read at a funeral, which I did when I served as a chaplain at a hospice and officiated at a couple of funerals. Certainly, this is one interpretation; however, understanding John 14:1–3 only as a promise for Heaven after we die is like receiving a crumb when a bountiful feast is available to us or being gifted a beautiful home and told we cannot move into it until the end of our lives.

Let's address the first interpretation of being home/in Heaven with Jesus when we die. It would help to read these verses:

> *"Do not let your hearts be troubled. Trust in God; trust also in me. In my Father's house are many rooms; if it were not so, I would have told you. I am going there to prepare a place for you. And if I go and prepare a place for you, I will come back and take you (receive-ASV) to be with me, that you also may be where I am. 23b My Father will love him* (those who love Jesus), *and we will come to him and make our home with him."*

It is always important to understand verses in their context. These words were given by Jesus to comfort and instruct His disciples during what we refer to as the Upper Room Discourse before His death and resurrection. This would be the final, critical message He wanted them to understand, so it carries much weight. He has been telling them that He will be leaving them, so from their human understanding it makes sense that they would be grieving and troubled. Jesus understands their sadness; yet, He tells them not to be troubled. If the promise for His return would be only for the far distant future of Heaven, then their grief would be completely appropriate. Just like we grieve when our loved ones in Christ die, even though we have the promise of being reunited with them in Heaven.

So, what did Jesus mean when he told His disciple that there was no need for troubled hearts or grief? When we interpret the Bible through our English language we tend to miss its original meaning and the way His disciples would have understood His words. So let's look at the Greek meaning. The word "house"—(a noun) means "residence, an abode, by implication, a family home, household." The Greek for "many rooms" (verb) really means "a staying, residence; to stay in a given place, state, relation, abide." The two words are virtually the same and would have been understood by the disciples as Jesus, in essence, saying, I am going to prepare a place in my Father's house (the Temple), in which you will be part of our household and given an abiding, continuing relationship. I will be providing greater detail on *abiding* in a future chapter.

Wow, it is **not** a big room in a fancy mansion, but a "household," or in our language, family relationship. Jesus was saying that He was leaving (going to die) and returning (resurrected) to prepare a place in His Father's household or family. So, do we wait until we are in Heaven to be with Him and to become part of the family of God? The answer is "No", we become/became God's child, Jesus' brother or sister and part of the family of God at the time of salvation. So then, when Jesus said *"'I will come back and take you (receive-NAS) to be with me, that you also may be where I am,"* He is talking about His resurrection, and our acceptance in faith of this truth. He receives us into His family to be with and in His presence, His household at the moment of salvation. From this time forward, there is now no separation between Him and us.

Oh what joy and good news this is. I can remember the great joy I experienced when I realized that we already have our eternal home, in Christ, *now*. Yes, we still groan and wait with all creation for the total redemption of our bodies and still struggle with all the heartache and troubles of this world, but I don't have to wait to be made complete or have Jesus' presence. Also, the idea of looking forward to a "mansion" in Heaven always seemed so materialistic; whereas, being part of God's eternal household is far more appealing and true to the Father's heart.

Now let's take a closer look at the second interpretation sometimes applied to the John 14 verses when Jesus said: *"I will come back and take you to be with me."* These words have sometimes been interpreted to mean that we will be taken (received) to be with Him at His second coming, which is referenced in Matthew 24 and 25. The terms Jesus used in these two passages are very different. In John 14:1—4, Jesus used the word "receive (NAS)." The Greek definition for *"receive"* is "to receive near, i.e. *associate with oneself (in a familiar or intimate act or relation,)* In Matthew 24 and 25, in which Jesus is talking about His "second coming" or return from Heaven the second time, He uses terms such as *"gather together," "one will be taken, and one will be left"* Matt 24:40—41. The Greek meaning of the words, *"gather together"* are; "to collect upon the same place." This difference in meaning also make it clear that Jesus' words and promise in John speak about bringing us into an intimate, personal relationship with Him and not the time when we will be taken up and gathered together out of this world at the end of the age (His second coming).

So the question is, how might the two misinterpretations impact our lives? One possible way is to understand a situation in which parents leave their child with a caretaker, promise to be back soon, and do not return for a long time. I believe this would create a great deal of anxiety and fear, breaking trust, which would cause the child to doubt and lose faith. Look at the words Jesus uses to give assurance: *"If it were not so, I would have told you."* (John 14:2) — He is telling us that we can fully believe and trust Him. He longs for us to experience all the blessings and joy He has gained for us through His sacrifice. You see, those who have received Jesus, or rather have been received by Him, have nothing to fear and don't have to wait in anxiety for His second return. We are fully part of His family and completely belong to Him. Now that is "good news." I can joyfully, trustingly, peacefully abide in His presence right here and now and fully enjoy all our heavenly Father has given me in the amazing gift of His salvation. Let these words from Galatians 4:4–5 sink deep into your heart, mind, and soul: "… *God sent his Son, born of a women, born under law, to redeem those under law,* **that we might receive the full rights of sons** *(emphasis added). Because you are sons, God sent the Spirit of his Son into our hearts, the Spirit who calls out, 'Abba, Father.'"* God has given us all the riches, blessings, and gifts of His presence to enjoy, and in which we can feel secure.

In addition to losing out on the joy of His salvation, we are in danger of getting sidetracked by all the troubles of this world. Like that child waiting for the parent's return, we are far more likely to act out in our anxiety and get into trouble. In addition we are more vulnerable to Satan's temptations of building our own kingdom on earth. Isn't that precisely what we end up doing? Going back to the verses in Matthew 24: 45–49, which speak of His second coming, it is interesting that Jesus used a parable to warn us of this very thing: *"Who then is the faithful and wise servant, whom the master has put in charge of the servants in his household to give them their food at the proper time?... But suppose that servant is wicked and says to himself, 'My master is staying away a long time,' and he then begins to beat his fellow servants and to eat and drink with drunkards."* This may be an extreme example; however, all of us know that we struggle with temptations, anxiety, fear, and all kinds of relational difficulties as a result of not walking closely in the presence of Jesus.

If we do not realize that Jesus has already received us and is completely present with us, we tend to focus solely on ourselves and forget to live our life to glorify Him, who is our Master, King, Savior, and Lord. Colossians 3:1–3 states it this way: *"Since, then, you have been raised with Christ, set your hearts on things above, where Christ is seated at the right hand of God. Set your minds on things above, not on earthly things. For you died, and your life is now hidden with Christ in God."* Nothing will steal away our joy more than getting our eyes off Jesus and focusing on the kingdom of this world, our self-interests, and troubling circumstances.

We all live afflicted and conflicted lives while we wait for God's final redemptive work (our new bodies in His new Heaven and Earth).

This is why the prayer in Psalm 51:10, 12 starts with these words: ***"Create in me a pure heart, O God, and renew a steadfast spirit within me... Restore to me the joy of your salvation and grant me a willing spirit, to sustain me"*** (emphasis added). In other words, we cannot produce joy by making our life happy and comfortable; joy is not based on circumstances but is a direct result of living a life that is rightly connected with God and a gift or fruit of His Spirit. I will be addressing this at greater length later in this book. I pray your mind has been renewed and that you may begin to enjoy His presence/home now.

CHAPTER 2
DO YOU STRUGGLE TO FEEL GOD'S PRESENCE?

I just spent a whole chapter discussing John 14:1–4 as one of the reasons we don't feel Jesus'/God's presence and joy in our lives. Yet there are additional reasons for this struggle. How often have you prayed, "God be with me in this situation," or heard others pray for God to be with a specific person or situation? Most of us are very familiar with God's promise, in Old and New Testament, in which He says, "Never will I leave you, never will I forsake you" (Dt. 3:16; Josh. 1:5; 2Chr. 15:2; Ps. 27:10; Heb. 13:5). So, the question then becomes, Why do I feel distance and absence from Him, or why do I feel the need to ask Him to be with me? And if I don't feel His presence, then how can I be filled with His joy, when He says, "you will fill me with joy in your presence" (Ps. 16:11)? For many years I also struggled to feel His presence. But God has worked in my life over the past few years and given me the insights to understand the reasons for this struggle. In this chapter I would like to share some of these insights. This does not mean that I don't occasionally feel distant from Him, but I experience His presence far more easily and consistently.

Let's begin with the most common reason that we pray for Him to be "with us." It may simply be a habit and the way we have heard everyone pray in church. It is the pattern we follow blindly without thinking of the words we are really saying to our heavenly Father.

A second possible reason is that we have not quieted our hearts and minds to come into His presence and not given Him our full attention. We may just be so busy in our minds and doing all the talking to Him that we are not even really conscious of the fact that He may have something to say to us. He helped me to understand this more deeply by giving me the analogy of our closest relationships on earth. All too often we fall into the trap of being with someone, yet not really listening to them, or focusing on what their need may be. We may live with them physically but not really know their heart and soul. Unity and closeness cannot thrive in such situations, which ends up robbing us of the deepest joy in relationship. Yet, do we stop for one minute to realize that (probably unintentionally) we do precisely the same to our heavenly Father? By asking Him to be with us we are indirectly accusing Him of not being with us, when we are the ones not giving our full attention to Him. Just like in our closest relationship, we grieve the Holy Spirit with whom we are one and are robbed of joy. Our joy is complete when His joy is complete.

So, to address these two shortcomings, try picturing Him next to you as you give full attention to Him. You may want to say something like this: "Thank you Father God that You are with me, that You never leave me or forsake me. Help me to quiet my mind and draw near to You so I can hear Your voice; open my heart to see and feel your presence." Or if you are praying for others, pray "that they may know and experience His presence." The prayer from Ephesians 3:14–19 is also effective and appropriate.

The third possible reason we don't experience God's presence and therefore miss out on the joy of His salvation, may be un-repented sin. The beginning of Psalm 51:10, from which the title of this book comes, starts with a request for God to *"Create in me a clean heart, O God."* This verse makes it clear that before we can experience the joy of His salvation, we need to have a clean heart. We are not rejected or abandoned by our heavenly Father because we have sinned. However, just like in our earthly relationships, unity and intimate fellowship is broken when we sin against one another. If our un-repented sin is not addressed and confessed, it causes a rift in our relationship and hinders our ability to experience God's presence. He has not withdrawn from us; we just are unable to feel His loving presence. This is true in both our earthly and spiritual relationships.

This truth was recently impressed upon me in a new way. I had been at odds with my husband over an issue. We had difficulty coming to terms after a brief conversation. I began realizing how miserable I felt when there was tension and conflict between us. I didn't want to be close to him at that moment, yet I hated the distance I felt between us. The marriage wasn't dissolved because of our disagreement, but the unity and closeness was. As I meditated on this, I realized that this is what happens when the unity is broken between my heavenly Father, Jesus, and myself. God does not reject and abandon, or disown us because of sin, but it hinders our closeness and unity with Him. We miss out on the joy of His presence.

So in this situation our prayer needs to be *"search my heart and see if there be any offensive way in me* (Ps 139:23). In order to restore the joy and unity, we need to take time to listen and understand how we have sinned and grieved the Holy Spirit of God and caused the distance, and to confess it.

I just pointed out that sin could be the cause for us to feel distant from God, but that He does not rejects us. However, I wonder how many of us believe and feel that God actually does forsake us, turn away from us, or punish us when we sin and therefore do not want to draw near and even fear His presence? One reason you may feel that way is because you may have, sadly, been victims of conditional love, which is based on performance and says, "If you please me, I will give you the love and affection, but if you don't, I will deny you my love and attention and will punish you." If we have been abused, we come to believe that all love is conditional and based on performance, even though we are taught from the Bible that God's love is unconditional. Unknowingly we are trapped in one of Satan's many lies to keep us feeling distant from the One who loves us unconditionally, which adds to our pain and leaves us hopeless, despairing, immobilized, and running further from God's true heart of love, mercy, and grace. This mistaken belief has deep consequences in our spiritual walk and creates a bigger distance between us and our Abba (Daddy).

From the beginning of time, God's purpose has been to enjoy an intimate, loving relationship with us, and to enable us to know and enjoy His loving presence. Listen to St. Paul's words in Ephesians 1:3–4: *"Praise be to the God and Father of our Lord Jesus Christ, who has blessed us in the heavenly realms with every spiritual blessing in Christ… In love He predestined us to be adopted as His sons through Jesus Christ."* I pray as you continue to read, that your mind would be renewed and God's truth will set you free.

Another reason we may feel distant from God and struggle to feel His presence is when we are in great distress and emotional or physical pain. There are several verses in Psalms in which the psalmist cries out to God and feels abandoned or forsaken because of his painful circumstances, as in Psalm 31:22: *In my alarm I said, 'I am cut off from your sight?' Yet you heard my cry for mercy when I called to you for help."* We are also familiar with Jesus' words on the cross, when He cried out to His Father these piercing words: *"My God, my God, why have you forsaken me?"* (Mark 15:34) So let's look at what happens when we are in pain.

What We Experience When We Suffer

When we are in great pain we usually feel very alone and isolated; we struggle to make sense of why; we want nothing more than for the suffering to end quickly. We feel like no one really understands what we are going through, and, at times, accuse them of not being supportive. All our energy is focused on minimizing the pain and finding peace. In our helpless condition we are vulnerable to Satan's lies, darkness, hopelessness, and depression. Whether that suffering is due to sin or the result of living in a diseased, fallen world, our deepest need and desire at that time is for assurance, compassion, understanding, and the tangible support of another. This is true of each of us, and it was true of Jesus, who experienced this same sense of abandonment while hanging on the cross. He acutely felt separated from the Father. But is it true that God and others abandon us when we suffer? Or do our feelings deceive and blind us to the truth?

I believe our loved ones usually rally around us and lend whatever support they can. If we see our loved one hurting, we do all we can, short of rescuing them from the situation, just because we love them. The truth is we do draw near to them; we share in their pain and grief and often feel their pain acutely. Likewise, our heavenly Father, Who is love and only capable of love, does the same for His own beloved children. How do we know this? Because we see times in Jesus' life when He wept with and over those grieving (John 11:17–35). We also are admonished to *"weep with those who weep"* (Romans 12:15). These truths would not be given to us if they didn't represent the nature and heart of our heavenly Father.

Just recently, I was reminded of this truth. We have been carrying the stress and grief with our son and his family while he was let go from a job and going on interview after interview. As his parents, we would feel the rise and fall of hope and despair. My prayers for them would fluctuate between total faith, hope, and trust in God to feeling utter discouragement and asking "Why?" telling God that we just don't understand. Yet in the midst of this long ordeal I would feel Abba's gentle touch and loving presence. The greatest comfort came when one very dark morning as I wept for my son, I heard Abba's voice speak to my heart, saying, "I am weeping with you. Just like you are weeping for your children, I am weeping with you." Hearing this didn't take away the pain or the feeling like I couldn't breathe, but somehow I no longer felt alone in the pain. This brought some measure of comfort.

You see, our heavenly Father is not distant, uncaring, unfeeling, rejecting, or untouched by our grief. I believe He feels our pain and stands with us in it. But in those moments of deep despair, our feelings overwhelm our understanding, and our knowledge of God becomes clouded. The difficulty for us is that we do not see and know all as God does, which is why drawing near to Abba in our deepest times of pain and distress is most important. It is only then that we will be able to hear our loving heavenly Father's voice of comfort and get to know His heart. One of my favorite songs expresses this truth—

Trust His Heart

All things work for our good, though sometimes we don't see how they could.
Struggles that break our hearts in two, sometimes blind us to the truth.
Our Father knows what's best for us; His ways are not our own.
So when your pathway grows dim and you just don't see Him, remember you're never alone.
(Chorus) God is too wise to be mistaken; God is too good to be unkind.
So when you don't understand; when you can't trace His hand, trust His heart.[1]

As we continue exploring the interaction between Jesus and His disciples that last night in the upper room, we will see how their lack of understanding caused so much of their distress. The disciples had been with Jesus for three years, yet it appears they did not really know Jesus or understand His mission.

CHAPTER 3
JESUS: THE WAY, TRUTH, AND LIFE

John 14:4-9

After Jesus provided hope and comfort to His despairing disciples by assuring them of His return and presence, the night before His death, He continues the dialog with them in John 14:3–7. These are equally critical verses, which also impact our walk with Him. Let's look more deeply at His words:

"'And if I go and prepare a place for you, I will come back and take you to be with me that you also may be where I am. You know the way to the place where I am going.' Thomas said to him, 'Lord, we don't know where you are going, so how can we know the way?' Jesus answered, **'I am the way, and the truth, and the life. No one comes to the Father except through me** (emphasis added). If you really knew me, you would know my Father as well. From now on, you do know him and have seen him.'"

It is clear from these verses that the disciples were totally overwhelmed and confused during this last supper. They didn't fully understand all Jesus came to do or what was about to happen. Unfortunately, at times we suffer with the same lack of understanding. For many years I had a limited understanding of the John 14:6 verse, in which Jesus told them He is *"the way, the truth, and the life."* I always believed these words referred only to Him as being the way of salvation to the Father. Certainly, they mean that; however, is that all they mean? From what I have learned, I don't believe so, which I will attempt to share with God's help. Understanding these verses as Jesus meant them has brought incredible joy and depth to my walk with Him.

I want you to notice the grammatical tense in which Jesus made the statement: *"'I am the way and the truth and the life. No one comes to the Father except through me.'"* First of all, Jesus says of Himself, "*I am*"—My very personhood, not the historical facts and information about me. Second, the words, "*am*" and "*comes*," are present tense, active; an ongoing, active reality. He did not say, *I will be or I was*. Nor does He say, no one *came or will come*. By expressing Himself in the present tense He is saying He is currently, presently, and continually still the *only way, truth, and life* to the Father. He is describing a life of absolute dependency upon Himself, and the sole vehicle through whom we enter and maintain a relationship with the Father. We approach the Father through Jesus, we can only know the Father through Jesus, and we can only live the life of the Father in Jesus. Do we seek His counsel on every decision? Do we realize that each day given to us is not ours but given to us to

ABIDING

do His work in and through Christ? As St. Paul wrote, *"You are not your own; you were bought with a price."* (I Cor. 6:19b). Jesus is the Alpha and Omega, the beginning and the end, a continuum.

Do I Look to Jesus as the Author and Perfecter of My Faith?

The idea that once we are saved (born again) we can just run our lives as we wish is troublesome, grievous, and a deception from the world, flesh, and the devil. It makes no sense and is analogous to either giving birth to a child and just abandoning it or having a wonderful, happy wedding day and then forsaking our mate and living life as a single person. Would we enjoy the blessings of a child or marriage if we made such a choice? In both examples, failure to thrive would be the obvious result. The Father united Himself to us through Christ so that we *"may have life and have it to the full"* (abundantly, John 10:10). He planned a life with and in Him eternally, continually, living as **one**. This is His deepest desire and the reason He first created mankind and then paid the incredible price of sending His Son as the sacrifice to bring us back to Himself. But it can only happen if we rely on Jesus as the way, the truth, and the source of life, and keep our eyes on Him.

Hebrews 12:1–3 states this truth in the following way:

> *"Therefore, since we are surrounded by such a great cloud of witnesses, let us throw off everything that*

hinders and the sin that so easily entangles, and let us run with perseverance the race marked out for us. Let us fix our eyes on Jesus, the author and perfecter of our faith, who for the joy set before him endured the cross, scorning its shame, and sat down at the right hand of the throne of God. Consider him who endured such opposition from sinful men, so that you will not grow weary and lose heart."

This Scriptures makes it clear that salvation is just the beginning, and that our Father desires us to stay with Him to know Him. But like the disciples demonstrated in the John 14 dialog with Jesus, although they had been with Him for three years, they still didn't fully know Him. Let's go back to this conversation between Jesus and Phillip.

He asks Philip, *"Have I been so long with you, and yet you have not come to know Me, Philip?* Can you hear the grief in His voice? I can hear Him say the same to me and to many of us. We have *come to Him* through faith and accepted Him as *the only way* of salvation to the Father. We have, possibly been a Christian for many years, yet do we really *know* Him? Do we realize the source and growth of our faith is Jesus' life in us?

This is Oswald's insight into Jesus' words to Phillip, as stated in John 14.

These words were not spoken as a rebuke, nor even with surprise; Jesus was encouraging Philip to draw closer. Yet the last person we get intimate with is Jesus. Before Pentecost the disciples knew Jesus as the One who gave them power to conquer demons and to bring about a revival (see Luke 10:18–20). It was a wonderful intimacy, but there was a much closer intimacy to come: "… I have called you friends…" (John 15:15). True friendship is rare on earth. It means identifying with someone in thought, heart, and spirit. The whole experience of life is designed to enable us to enter into this closest relationship with Jesus Christ. We receive His blessings and know His Word, but do we really know Him?

Jesus said, "It is to your advantage that I go away…" (John 16:7). He left that relationship to lead them even closer. It is a joy to Jesus when a disciple takes time to walk more intimately with Him. The bearing of fruit is always shown in Scripture to be the visible result of an intimate relationship with Jesus Christ (see John 15:1–4). [1]

As I write these words, I am painfully aware of my own failure to consistently walk in the knowledge of this truth. The battle becomes in knowing the truth in our heads and living it out with our heart. We have the world, the flesh, and the devil constantly at our heels derailing us. It is a battle that we cannot win without the indwelling power of Christ, and a battle that will leave us exhausted, disillusioned, and discouraged. We question, "Where is the promised peace, rest, and joy?" So I pray Paul's words will encourage you—*"Let us not become weary in doing good, for at the proper time we will reap a harvest if we do not give up."* (Galatians 6:9). I also hope this book is the beginning of fulfilling what St. Paul wrote in Romans 12:2: *"Do not conform any longer to the pattern of this world, but be transformed by the renewing of your mind. Then you will be able to test and approve what God's will is—his good pleasing and perfect will."*

CHAPTER 4
HOW DO WE TAKE HOLD OF THE PEACE AND REST OF CHRIST?

John 14:27

Jesus repeatedly spoke of and promised His peace to His disciples. In John 14:27, He says, *"Peace I leave with you; my peace I give you."* So, do you find yourself asking for that peace and questioning why you experience your life in Christ as an endless, exhausting, battle? The book of Hebrews tells us,

> *"Therefore, since the promise of entering His rest still stands, let us be careful that none of you be found to have fallen short of it. For we also have had the gospel preached to us, just as they did; but the message they heard was of no value to them, because those who heard did not combine it with faith. Now we who have believed enter that rest,... There remains, then, a Sabbath-rest for the people of God; for anyone*

who enters God's rest also rests from his own work,…
Let us, therefore, make every effort to enter that rest".
(Hebrews 4:1–11)

The rest the Scripture speaks of here is ceasing our efforts to earn God's favor, love, and righteousness, as well as resting (totally relying on) Christ to live a life honoring our heavenly Father.

The verse that God used to help me embrace this life of rest more fully was Matthew 11:28–30. It reads as follows: *"'Come to me, all you who are weary and burdened, and I will give you rest. Take my yoke upon you and learn from me, for I am gentle and humble in heart, and you will find rest for yours souls. For my yoke is easy and my burden is light.'"* I am aware that there have been many sermons taught on these verses; never the less, I feel led to include a discussion of them. To begin this discussion, I need to share a personal experience I had the morning of writing this part of the book and was the catalyst for including it.

I was having my special time with my Father first thing in the morning while my husband was still sleeping. I did my usual reading of several devotionals and then the suggested reading in Luke for the Sunday's service. As I was reading, I suddenly realized two things: first, I was just reading to get the reading done; second I was not really reading to hear His voice—not really being present to Him in the reading. I was *not* "coming to *Him*." This happens all too often.

A little later that morning, as I was walking on the beach by myself, I became aware that my eyes kept tearing up. There was no physical reason for it—no wind blowing in my face, no rain, and no pain or irritation in my eyes. It was a calm day. I sensed His presence very strongly and then heard God's still voice saying, "The tears are mine." So I asked over what He was grieving. He began speaking to me; showing me that His grief was over the very subject from this morning—"coming to Him." Since I am a visual learner He frequently will teach me through word pictures or parables or spiritual visions (like a moving picture in my mind, but perceived and understood only by my spirit). There were two different images.

In the first, I saw two people in the ocean. One was someone who was drowning, panicked, very fearful. The other was Jesus. Jesus was in front of the person, fairly close but not touching, with His hands stretched out to the person. He repeatedly said, "Come to Me; just come to Me and take My hand. I will save you. You are getting weary and exhausted by fighting the waves in your attempt to save yourself. You will drown if you do not come to Me." But the person would not trust and come to Him but kept trying to get to safety on their own, believing he could eventually save himself. Jesus, with tears in His eyes, explained that this image was, as we can all guess, of one who is resisting "coming to Him" for salvation. Many of us have interpreted Matthew 11:28 to mean coming to Jesus for our salvation. And it does. However, Jesus has taught me that there is

HOW DO WE TAKE HOLD OF THE PEACE AND REST OF CHRIST?

far more to these verses, which have a greater impact on those of us already Christians, as given in the second image.

In the second image there were again two people in the ocean with big waves and no land nearby. Jesus was holding the other person from behind. But the person kept fighting, twisting and turning to be released from the arms around him/her. Jesus was saying, "Just rest in my arms, surrender, and relax. Trust Me, I've got you. I will bring you to safety." However, the person kept looking around for something (one) else to help because they didn't know this being, and didn't know if they could trust him.

Jesus explained the meaning of this image, as one who is saved but repeatedly turns to things other than Him to have peace, safety, hope, and happiness. When the image was done, I felt the deep sadness of Jesus and my Father. He is our rest, strength, joy, peace, wisdom, sound mind, and provision. Jesus fought, won, and overcame every battle we face on this earth, and all we need do is rest in His arms. In Hebrews we are told that He identifies with every grief because He was tested and tried as we are (Hebrews 4:14–16). He grieves over us as we struggle in our hopelessness, despair, frustration, anxiety, depression, anger, strife, addictions, and isolation,

I believe all of us have the tendency to rely on and trust in things like a spouse, job, money, drugs, family, parents, friends, pastor, the church, doctors, a vacation, or the government to be okay, feel better, be happy, and to have peace and rest. These can easily become **idols.** For two reasons, they take the place God rightfully deserves as our

ABIDING

primary source of help and strength. Second, if our eyes are on these other things then we are not focused on and pulling with Jesus to accomplish His work. While we are preoccupied with looking to other sources for help and trying to control our situations and others in the belief that these will save us and lighten our overwhelming burdens, our Savior is holding us and saying, *"Come to me, all you who are weary and burdened, and I will give you rest... learn from me, for I am gentle and humble in heart, and you will find rest for your souls.'"* Learning, by its very definition, means, staying long enough, remaining, focusing, being humble, and recognizing a need to learn. It involves an ongoing relationship of dependence. For those of you who have known me, it is my favorite word and subject—ABIDING.

Are My Eyes on Jesus or on Idols?

Oswald Chambers expresses the tendency to rely on things other than God as idols in the following words:

Lift up your eyes on high,... —Isaiah 40:26

> The people of God in Isaiah's time had blinded their minds' ability to see God by looking on the face of idols... Is your mind focused on the face of an idol? Is the idol yourself? Is it your work? Is it your idea of what a servant should be, or maybe your experience of

salvation and sanctification? If so, then your ability to see God is blinded... It is God you need. Go beyond yourself and away from the faces of your idols and away from everything else that has been blinding your thinking. Wake up... and deliberately turn your thoughts and your eyes to God... The power of visualization is what God gives a saint so that he can go beyond himself and be firmly placed into relationships he never before experienced.[1]

(This last sentence gives me encouragement, since I often feel I border on insanity when I experience God's teaching and speaking through various images and visions.). By using Oswald's quote I don't want you to be thinking that visualization is the only way that God speaks. The point I want to stress is to look to God for wisdom and direction.

Going back to the issue of idols, does it mean that it is wrong for us to rely on those blessings God has given us? We know from Scripture that our heavenly Father encourages and wants us to come to Him with all our needs. As stated previously, it often is our need that brings us to Him. God can speak to us through books, music, counselors, pastors, fellow believers, parents, TV programs, doctors, and so on to provide answers and encouragement. So the source is not the problem. However, the problem is when we see the other (person, job, doctor, friend, husband, pastor, winning the lottery, the new car) as the *thing* that will bring us happiness, wholeness, and peace. We have the tendency to depend on these other objects/blessings in our lives instead of coming to Jesus with our decisions to seek Him and His counsel. What does Proverbs tell us? *"Trust in the LORD with all your heart and lean not on your own understanding; in all your ways acknowledge him, and he will make your paths straight"* (Prov. 3:5–6). Notice that we are to *first* trust in the personhood of God who will then provide the wisdom and guidance we need. I have learned over time to take what I hear from human sources to Jesus and my Father to get their thoughts and perspective. The times I have failed to do this, which happens all too often, I have regrets and have to live with poor choices.

These are Henri Nouwen's words of wisdom on this subject: "Our desire for God is the desire that should guide all other desires. Otherwise, our bodies, minds, hearts, and wills become one another's enemies, and our inner lives become chaotic, leading to despair and self-destruction."[2] This is precisely what Jesus was telling us in the Matthew 11 verses: we can feel burdened, confused, overwhelmed, and filled with anxiety when we look for help to sources other than God. We prize independence, self-reliance, strength, and intellectual knowledge. But the "rest for our souls" promised here depends upon keeping totally connected to and our attention focused on Christ (yoked to Him).

Chambers writes this on the Matthew 11 verses:

> God intends for us to live a well-rounded life in Christ Jesus, but there are times when that life is attacked from the outside... . Yet it is never God's will that we should be anything less than absolutely complete in Him. Anything that disturbs our rest in Him must be rectified at once, and it is not rectified by being ignored, but only by coming to Jesus Christ. If we will come to Him, asking Him to produce Christ-awareness in us, He will always do it, until we fully learn to abide in Him.
>
> Never allow anything that divides or destroys the oneness of your life with Christ to remain in your life without facing it. Beware of allowing the influence of your friends or your circumstances to divide your life. This only serves to sap your strength and slow your spiritual growth. Beware of anything that can split your oneness with Him, causing you to see yourself as separate from Him. Nothing is as important as staying right spiritually. And the only solution is a very simple one—"Come to Me..." [3]

ABIDING

So how do we recognize when we have made our blessings an idol? The way my Father has helped me to identify this possible trap is by examining my heart to see if I am willing to put the thing on which I depend on God's altar. In other words, if God asks me to give up something or someone, am I willing to obey? This concept comes from the book of Genesis, in which God asked Abraham to take his son— *"your only son, Isaac, whom you love"*—a son miraculously, born of promise and grace and *"Sacrifice him there as a burnt offering"* (Genesis 22:2, the account recorded in verses 1–19). This Scripture is for many a difficult and problematic story, but if understood from God's perspective, it is a powerful account in which Abraham's faith and faithfulness was tested by God to determine whether he would place God above anything (one) else. God was asking Abraham, "Am I really above all else in your life, even the greatest gift of your son?" This is the question we need to answer as well. Even though, many of the blessings we have are good things and gifts from God, we need to be careful not to place them as a higher priority to God. It takes the divine wisdom of the Holy Spirit to discern the answer.

In the Gospel of Luke 11:11–13 we are told, *"'Which of you fathers, if your son asks for a fish, will give him a snake instead?...If you then, though you are evil, know how to give good gifts to your children, how much more will your Father in heaven give the Holy Spirit to those who ask him.'"* This verse tells me that our heavenly Father desires to provide for our needs, but more than anything we need the Holy Spirit. We *need Jesus'* presence in our lives to have complete fulfillment and discernment on whether we are seeking happiness, relief, peace, and rest from God, the giver of all good gifts, or the gifts themselves. So, this is why we need to hear Him say, "Come to me," in all the trials and difficult, overwhelming, painful situations, stresses of life, overpowering societal pressure for success, wealth, and things.

Jesus lived this same life of dependency on the Father, as these words communicate: *"The words I say to you are not just my own. Rather, it is the Father, living in me, who is doing his work'"* (John 14:10.) If Jesus did not, and could not accomplish the work of His Father without total dependency and connectedness, then why do we think we can? So He is the only one who can and should teach us and enable us to live that same life. This was what He meant with His words in Matthew. He will not force us to be yoked to Him and learn from Him. His words are an *invitation*. But, sadly, in our pride and self-determination, we exhaust ourselves trying to survive. And so there He is with tears in His eyes, waiting patiently for us to turn to Him for this rest. Just like Jesus wept over Jerusalem when He saw its pain and turmoil as written in Luke 19:41, 42, *"As he approached Jerusalem and saw the city, he wept over it and said, 'If you, even you, had only known on this day what would bring you peace.'"* ... He wept then, He weeps now over our unwillingness to *"come to Him."*

Speaking of this passage in Luke, Oswald Chambers challenges us with these words:

What is it that blinds you to the peace of God "in this *your* day"? Do you have a strange god—not a disgusting monster but perhaps an unholy nature that controls your life? More than once God has brought me face to face with a strange god in my life, and I knew that I should have given it up, but I didn't do it. I got through the crisis "by the skin of my teeth," only to find myself still under the control of that strange god. I am blind to the very things that make for my own peace. It is a shocking thing that we can be in the exact place where the Spirit of God should be having His completely unhindered way with us, and yet we only make matters worse, increasing our blame in God's eyes.

"If you had known…" God's words here cut directly to the heart, with the tears of Jesus behind them. These words imply responsibility for our own faults. God holds us accountable for what we refuse to see or are unable to see because of our sin. And "now they are hidden from your eyes" because you have never completely yielded your nature to Him. Oh, the deep, unending sadness for what might have been![4]

May we learn from Him and ask Him to open the eyes of our hearts. Coming to Him in prayer, knowing Him through the Word, and loving

Him through the power of His indwelling Spirit are the many ways we experience the *joy of His salvation*.

I close this chapter with the words of this song:

<u>Oceans Where Feet May Fail</u>

You call me out upon the waters
The great unknown where feet may fail
And there I find You in the mystery
In oceans deep my faith will stand.
Chorus: And I will call upon Your name
And keep my eyes above the waves
When oceans rise my Soul will rest in your embrace
For I am Yours and You are mine.

Your grace abounds in deepest waters
Your sovereign hand will be my guide
Where feet may fall and fear surrounds me
You've never failed and you won't start now.
Chorus: And I will call upon your name, etc

Spirit lead me where my trust is without borders
Let me walk upon the waters wherever You would call me
Take me deeper than my feet could ever wander
And my faith will be made stronger in the presence of my Savior[5]

CHAPTER 5
THE JOY OF **THE WORD**

John 1:1–14

For many years the written Word, psalms, and spiritual songs have been a source of great blessing, comfort, guidance, and strength. Yet, my Christian life continued to be more of a battle and source of frequent shame and discouragement. There were wonderful moments of peace and joy, but these seemed fleeting. It was only after my loving heavenly Father opened my understanding about His Word that I began experiencing His presence and deeper, consistent joy and peace in my life. I have always heard the Scriptures (Bible) referred to as "the Word of God." Along with that reference, was the unspoken idea that the only way to hear God's voice was through reading the Scriptures. Now, by saying this, I am in no way negating the importance and power of the written Word. As 2 Timothy 3:16 states, *"All Scripture is God-breathed and is useful for teaching, rebuking, correcting and training in righteousness."* But I questioned if reading the Scriptures was the only way to hear God's voice, or can we dialog with Him the way he did with His disciples when He walked this earth? Are we limiting communication with Him by relying only on our Scripture reading?

In this chapter I'd like to share my new understanding and experiences of what Jesus taught me, and hopefully answer these questions. First, I want to provide the Greek meaning of the Word (logos): something said (including the thought); by impl. a topic (subject of discourse),... the **Divine Expression (i.e., Christ) (emphasis added)**:—account, cause, communication,... tidings." John 1:1–4, 14 also makes it clear that "the Word" is more than the Bible, so let's read it: *"In the beginning was the Word, and the Word was with God and the Word was God. He was with God in the beginning. Through him all things were made; without him nothing was made that has been made, and that life was the light of men... And the Word became flesh and made his dwelling among us.* Let's also look at 1 John 1:1–4:

> *"That which was from the beginning, which we have heard, which we have seen with our eyes, which we have looked at and our hands have touched—this we proclaim concerning* **the Word of life** *(emphasis added). The life appeared; we have seen it and testify to it, and we proclaim to you the eternal life, which was with the Father and has appeared to us... And*

> *our fellowship is with the Father and with his Son, Jesus Christ. We write this to make our joy complete."*

From both the Greek meaning and the above Scripture, it is apparent that the Word is both the written Scripture and Jesus, the living Word. It is also noteworthy, that Jesus always used the word "Scripture" when speaking of God's written word.

An additional Scripture God used to help me understand that the Word is more than just the written Scripture are the verses recorded in Jeremiah 31:31–34, which prophetically speak of Christ.

> *"'The time is coming,' declares the LORD, 'when I will make a new covenant with the house of Israel and with the house of Judah.... . This is the covenant I will make with the house of Israel after that time,' declares the LORD. 'I will put my law in their minds and write it on their hearts. I will be their God, and they will be my people. No longer will a man teach his neighbor, or a man his brother, saying, 'Know the LORD,' because they will all know me from the least of them to the greatest.'"*

As I understand these verses to mean, the Word, which is Christ in the form of the Spirit, is written (imprinted/permanently placed) on our hearts when we become born anew. This made it clear to me that I have His word with and in me at all times and can hear and know Him aside from reading the written Word. The freedom and joy I was able to experience with this new understanding, was amazing. I felt like I began to know Jesus and my Father on a much deeper, more intimate, level than before.

God once gave me a metaphor to help me better understand the truth of Jesus being the Word. Suppose I am in a love relationship, which started and grew via the Internet, and it was long distance. Through letters from my beloved I got to know him very well. My love grew and deepened to the point that we decided to marry and move in together. We would sit on the couch each morning or during the day, but instead of talking with my beloved face to face, I kept reading his letters, because I enjoyed the feeling I would get by reading about him and his love for me. As the days went by, I kept focusing on the letters. There were questions I had and wanted to better understand, but I kept going to the letters to see whether I could get the answers from them. Time passed. As we slowly grew apart, I noticed a sadness; the exciting feelings I used to get in reading the letters became less intense. I didn't feel like I really knew him very well or how to please the one I loved. Pleasing him became a duty rather than a pleasure. The joy, closeness, and excitement of the relationship faded.

We say that Christianity is a love relationship, which is what makes it distinct from other religions. Well, do we *really* apply that truth in our lives when we are limited to reading the Bible as the one and only source of knowing God's heart, or does it come by hearing Him speak, and having a love relationship? Hopefully the metaphor above has helped you get the picture. The Scripture is just that—a love letter from the One with whom we have a love relationship, which chronicles the history of that relationship. We often do get to know about Him and start building a relationship with Him through the writings of this letter (the Bible). Then we invite Him into our lives and are received by Him—move into the home together. But would we grow in our loving relationship if we simply kept reading letters about each other? The answer is obvious. The only way we grow in our love relationships is when we spend time with each other, sharing, listening deeply, working through misunderstandings, acknowledging one another, appreciating each other, and blessing each other's lives, communicating with each other our happiness and sadness as life brings joys and difficulties. I have come to realize that *is what Jesus, who is the Word, desires.* In addition, the danger is that reading the Bible can quickly become a duty instead of the joy of our salvation. Maybe, this is what Jesus meant when He spoke these words in Revelations 2:4: *"'I hold this against you: You have forsaken your first love.'"*

Jesus, in the form of the Holy Spirit, still desires to explain the Scriptures and, give us understanding of His words. He spoke these words to His disciples: *"Those who have ears to hear, let him hear."* In John 5:39 He said this to the religious leaders of His time: *"'You diligently study the Scriptures because you think that by them you possess eternal life. These are the Scriptures that testify about me, yet you refuse to come to me to have life.'"* Ouch!!! Do you hear the sadness in that statement? Can you see the correlation between those words and the analogy above? This is how Chambers expresses these same thoughts: "The vital relationship which the Christian has to the Bible is not that he worships the letter, but that the Holy Spirit makes the words of the Bible spirit and life to him." [1] It grieves me, and I believe Him, when our love relationship is just about taking a few moments in the day to read and pray.

As we read from the verses on joy at the very beginning of this book, the joy we experience is in His presence and in relationship with Him. We cannot experience the one without the other. I can personally testify to this. It is difficult to put into words what a difference and joy I have had in my relationship with my Father and Jesus since He opened my eyes and understanding of this truth. Now, I spend time throughout the day talking and trying to listen to Him. Like everyone, the listening is always the more difficult. It sometimes takes time to quiet my mind, but I can honestly say that I have gotten to know my Father and Brother Jesus and their hearts desires much more intimately. When I am with them I feel a touch of Heaven for brief moments. In my walks with Jesus, I have often felt the great joy of being taught and my eyes opened and my mind renewed about the Scriptures just like the account in the gospel of Luke 24:13–32, in which a couple of disciples were walking on the road to Emmaus and Jesus walked with. The last verse says, *"Their eyes were opened and they recognized him,... They asked each other, 'Were not our hearts burning within us while he talked with us on the road and opened the Scriptures to us?'"*

It is awesome and humbling to walk with Him even now, for He is still speaking and explaining the Scriptures, and helping us to know Him. This intimate relationship with Him is not for just a select few. He came, died, resurrected, ascended to the Father, and sent His Spirit so that all who believe can know and have this joyous relationship with Him.

Having shared all this, I don't want to give the impression that my life is devoid of painful struggle. The joy I experience is not due to life being a bed of roses. In fact, as I write this, one of our sons is facing the threat of divorce. A long-time friend is dying of cancer. I see the stress and strain of raising a family and making ends meet in the lives of all my three married children. So many burdens and battles weigh heavily on me as folks in our church family battle cancer, emotional issues, and broken relationships. There are wars and rumor of wars, untold human suffering. The pain is overwhelming at times, and I silently pray for Jesus to return. So the moments of joy are brief glimpses of Heaven and relief that help me bear the pain. But this is the very reason, I believe, my heavenly Father is moving me to write—it is His deep desire that all His beloved children share in this joy. It grieves Him when we don't receive and enjoy the rich blessings of life with and in Him.

A fellow traveler and mentor, Jim May, shares similar thoughts in his book *Black Ice*. "When you see the truth of our place in God, we begin to read God's Word in a new way. I hear Him speaking personally to me. The Word is not just dry words on a page, but living spirit in my heart."[2]

So now to get back to the question with which I started this chapter—does God only speak through the Scriptures, and is He still talking to us? Are we hearing Him when He is making Himself known? Hopefully, what I have written has given you a new understanding and a deeper hunger to be with Him and listen for His voice. However, I believe, there are additional reasons we have difficulty hearing our heavenly Father, reasons I'd like to discuss next.

Distracted by Many Things

First, and most likely, many of us are constantly busy with all the demands of this life and world. We seldom stop to be still to listen. I remember when I lived near the beach in California and was doing long daily walks in which I was communing with Jesus. I was learning so much about His heart and the abiding life. It was one of the most beautiful, impactful times in my life. Although, I was struggling with some of the most painful situations in my life, I felt the most joy and peace. The serenity of walking on the beach was a gift from Him, in which I could totally focus on Him.

ABIDING

These experiences remind me one of my favorite stories in the Bible, the one of Mary and Martha, found in Luke 10:38–42. Most likely you are very familiar with it—Martha is overwhelmed with taking care of the practical duties as hostess to Jesus and His disciples, while Mary (her sister) is sitting *"at the Lord's feet, listening to what he said."* I can so relate to this story, since it has frequently been a source of light-hearted banter between one of my three dear sisters, who is definitely a Martha, and myself. As you probably surmise, I am the Mary—I love nothing more than sitting (or walking, in my case) with Jesus and just listening to Him speak. Reading about Mary and Jesus' response to her choice—*"'Mary has chosen what is better, and it will not be taken away from her.'"*—has given me encouragement in the times when I am spending hours doing just that. However, when I am around my beloved sister, I start feeling guilty that I am not as active doing all the hospitable things needed. Sisters, by nature, have a tendency to make comparisons with one another. Between us, it has always just been light-hearted competition and not anything contentious. We have a deep love and mutual admiration for each other: I love, value, and admire her Martha qualities, and she values me as Mary. We bless one another with our gifts.

In the Luke account, I don't believe Jesus was saying that He loved one sister more than the other, or that the activity of one was of greater value. I believe the truth Jesus was trying to communicate in this story was that, in that moment of time and in this encounter, what was of greater importance for Him and them was sitting and listening at His feet. The point is, we have the tendency to get so distracted with all the pressures of this world that we neglect the things we need most—just being still and listening to Him speak. The only way we are ever going to hear and know our loved ones or God is if are quiet and completely focused. Hence this verse: *"Be still and know that I am God"*—Psalm 46:10. The Hebrew meaning of "be still" is "slacken, let it alone, cease striving," and "fail."

I have come to realize that by being with Him and listening, He is blessed and feels joy—the same joy I feel. If you are a Martha, be conscious of your need to give Jesus and yourself that time. On the other hand, if you are a Mary it may take greater focus on Jesus to be His hands and feet—being the doer.

Not only are we too busy, but we also are constantly listening to other's voices. When I was doing all those beach walks in California (mentioned previously) I observed that everyone I saw had earplugs in their ears and were listening to something or talking on their cell phones. It is as though we intentionally drown out God's still small voice with all the noise and activity.

The second possible reason we cannot hear our Father's voice is that we have so many resources available upon which we rely to answer our questions and struggles. Look at all the self-help books written on every possible problem we face. Then there is the Internet, reference books, magazines, and TV programs. I can go on and on. I am guessing that most pastors use other written resources, including reference books to prepare their messages. Now, I am not condemning use of those resources. Much of that material is very helpful to pastors, counselors, or teachers who have limited time and such demanding work schedules. But the point I am getting to is that all these resources are human knowledge, interpretations, accounts, experiences, and opinions. It is quicker and easier to rely on them instead of going directly to God for His understanding of the Scripture or opinions and solutions to our problems. In seeking help and answers from sources other than God, I fear, we too easily leave out ***the Healer, Redeemer, Counselor, Friend, Word of wisdom, and Prince of peace.***

This is Chamber's word of wisdom on this issue: "It is impossible to read too much, but always keep before you why you read. Remember that 'the need to receive, recognize, and rely on the Holy Spirit' is before all else."[4]

As I am writing these words, the fingers of accusation point right back to me. I fall short of walking this out in my life on a regular basis. So in order to provide a time for God/Holy Spirit/Jesus to talk to me, and to help me listen, I have adopted walks into my life (usually on a quiet nature trail). I visualize walking with Jesus, and I simply talk, listen, ask questions, work out my difficulties with Him, and try to see them from His perspective. Invariably, He will include a Scripture verse (reference) to testify to what I have heard, or He will ask me to look up additional Scripture as confirmation. (This is an important point: what we hear must never contradict the written Word, and it won't if it is from Him.) I want to stress that this is my way; I am not saying you have to do this. But, oh the joy that I feel when I am so connected with my Lord, Savior, Friend, Jesus.

Hearing Him through the "Parable of the Sower and the Soil"

I just discussed the importance of both reading and listening to the Word (Scripture and Jesus) in order to fully experience our Father's presence and joy. I also briefly wrote how the business of our lives often robs us of these blessings. Following is an example of this from my personal experience.

I was reading verses in Luke 8 as part of the suggested reading for our church. As I sat reading, I asked Jesus to give me a fresh insight into this parable. It is a parable with which many of us are very acquainted. So I wanted His insight and fresh application of it. The explanation didn't come right then but a little later as I was walking on the beach.

Before I share my experience it may be helpful to read this parable in Luke 8 and Mark 4: 3–20—"Parable of the Sower and the Soil," also named "the Parable of the Four Soils."

> *"A farmer went out to sow his seed. As he was scattering the seed, some fell along the path; it was trampled on, and the birds of the air ate it up. Some fell on rocky places, and when it came up, the plants withered because they had no moisture. Other seed fell*

> *among thorns, which grew up with it and choked the plants. Still other seed fell on good soil. It came up and yielded a crop, a hundred times more than was sown (NAS)."*

Most of the time this parable is interpreted to mean that the sowing of the seed is the *Word of God,* in which the seed is the gospel of salvation. The seed is either received or not, based upon the condition of the soil—the receptiveness of the human heart. I accept that is a correct application of those verses. But now I would like to challenge your minds by sharing another possible interpretation

In this explanation the sowing of the seed (Word) is sown into the lives of those who already are Christians. His Word can come to us in many different ways—a friend, sermon, the Scriptures, nature, circumstances. It can come as the still, small voice of our Savior (also known as the Holy Spirit). There is no specific time of day or place. Our hearts and ability to hear, listen, and receive God's truth depends on the condition of our hearts, minds, and souls. We can be so busy that our heart's condition is analogous to *"the path"* described in the parable. It didn't even receive the seed, because it was trampled on and the birds ate the seed. This is one who doesn't even go to church or spend time with Jesus or fellow Christians.

The second example is the rock upon which the seed fell but withered quickly. They are individuals who go to church, listen and agree and receive the word with joy, but it never really takes root in their lives. The third example is seed that fell among thorns. These are ones who go to church, fellowship with believers, read the Scriptures, but then their lives are taken over by the worry, fear, and business of the world's cares and burdens. They have no joy. The last is the good soil, which produces. This, obviously, is the Christian who hears, listens, and walks in the truths of Jesus. They have the vibrant, joyful, love relationship with Him and the Father and produce much fruit.

A couple of insights I would like to highlight from this passage. First, a specific time was not given in which the farmer (Jesus) went *"out to sow his seed."* It also did not state how long or where. The point I'd like to make here is that the time of day or length in which we sit and have our devotional time is not the critical issue for our spiritual growth. It needs to be when we are best able to be still and receive His word. God is far more concerned about the condition of our hearts and our openness to Him throughout the day. The second point is that the whole purpose of scattering the seed (the Word) is to produce fruit. It is clear from several other verses in Scripture that what God most cares about is producing fruit. John 15:8, 16: *"This is to my Father's glory that you bear much fruit, showing yourselves to be my disciples… You did not choose me, but I chose you and appointed you to go and bear fruit—fruit that will last."* I will be discussing the bearing of fruit at length in a future chapter.

Now I would like to share an experience I had as I was writing about the "Parable of the Sower", which God used to apply to my personal circumstances and encouraged me. I had been struggling again with writing this book, since I saw many of these ideas expressed in the readings of my daily devotionals. The first point Jesus highlighted was the fact that, the *"farmer went out to sow his seed"*; he simply did what he was destined to do. He did not first stop to inspect the soil before casting the seed, but simply spread it as he was going along. As is described, some fell on *"hard/rocky soil"* and some on *"good soil."* His responsibility was to sow (scatter) the seed, believing in faith it would produce. The second point is, it was not in the farmer's control to determine the outcome. This is how Jesus explained and applied this parable to my concerns of writing this book. It isn't for me to determine who will receive the content of this book (where it will be dispersed or the condition of the soil), nor the amount of fruit to grow out it. My sole responsibility is to sow (cast) the seed (the words written in this book) wherever it falls and let God decide the outcome. If I, or the farmer, stopped to figure out where the seed will fall or what it will produce, we would live in so much fear, that it never would be sent forth.

Immediately, after hearing this, I reaped the peace and joy of His sown Word into my life, and I could once again simply enjoy the writing, knowing that I don't have to worry about how much, or if, any fruit will be produced. That is totally in God's hands.

Jesus is often speaking, but are we listening? Are the cares of this world like the weeds or birds snatching away and choking the Word? The reason I believe the meaning of this parable applies to us who are already Christians and not just to the unsaved, is because the

Scripture says this: *"When he was alone, the Twelve and the others around him asked him about the parable. He told them, 'The secret of the kingdom of God has been given to you.'"* (Mark 4:10). Jesus, in the form of the Holy Spirit, is still speaking and is still explaining the Scriptures to us if, *"He who has ears to hear, (will) hear."*

To summarize, I believe we are blinded to and deprived of sharing much joy and blessing with our heavenly Father and Jesus by thinking of and applying the Word only as the written Scriptures, and not taking time out of our busy lives to be with Him and listen to Him. May you learn to experience Him with and in you in a new way, and fully enjoy the "joy of your salvation."

In the next chapter I would like to address some additional reasons we may struggle to feel close to our heavenly Father, feel the joy of His salvation, and hear His voice. The focus will be the following question: *Do we believe Jesus is actually with and in us now, or do we believe He is just a historical person who is our model and a good teacher?* We may believe Jesus came to earth in human form, died and resurrected to save us, and ascended to Heaven to be with the Father. We read the Scripture to see how He lived and ministered and then try to live like Him. He is the teacher and model whose life we try to emulate. But am I conscious of His living presence and does it make any difference?

CHAPTER 6
DO YOU BELIEVE JESUS IS ACTUALLY LIVING IN YOU?

The Promise of the Holy Spirit John 14:15-26

Since I became a Christian, I have studied the Scriptures and tried to live by their standards. It was a battle in which I often felt on the losing side. I didn't have much joy. Oh there were those occasional times of joy and feeling like I was connected to God, but it seemed more often than not, a big, long road of trial and error. It was after I had been a Christian thirty years, during a dark time in my life, that Christ opened my eyes to a truth in Scripture I had never really seen. Yes, I had read and studied the Scriptures many times, taught Sunday school, and led Bible studies; however, I had never really seen it with the eyes of my heart. This truth is that Jesus' living presence is in my life, and He is not just an external, historical person whom I'm supposed to be like. This may sound simplistic, and something we say even as children—Jesus is in my heart. But does the truth of this profound mystery really impact our lives?

Let me share this experience, which had a profound impact on my life—an encounter with Jesus, which caused me to feel born again, again. I share this with the cautionary note that it was my unique experience. Since God works uniquely in each of our lives, I am not saying you need to have this experience in order to know God and the abiding life.

It was a difficult time in my life. My husband and I had taken in my mother of ninety-six to live with us. Because she had Alzheimer's, much of what I had been able to do in church ministry had to be put on hold. During this time, I also felt hindered by my church from providing Christian counseling and restricted in the ministry of music, all of which were areas I believed God had gifted me to serve His body. I sank into a state of depression and felt very alone. I am not normally a depressed person. I have always been a pretty emotionally even-keeled person. I didn't want to share my burden with anyone (except my husband) for fear of being critical of leadership. So I could only talk with my heavenly Father about it, which I did over and over. I did all the things I normally did—pray, read, study the Bible, confess my sin—but nothing seemed to lift my spirit. I felt far from God. Each time I tried to pray and listen to His voice, all I would hear Him say would be, *"Be still and know that I am God."* (Ps 46:10) Frankly, I was tired of waiting, being still, and hearing Him speak those words. I didn't know what or how to pray any longer. I felt like I was in this deep, dark pit and no one cared that I was there. It was what St. John of the Cross referred to as "the dark night of the soul."[1]

Then one day, as I walked during my mom's nap, it seemed like the world around me faded into the background, and I was transported into a visionary world, in which I saw myself sitting on a rock in a desert, weeping. As I sat weeping, Jesus came, sat down next to me, put His arm around me, and said, "Maria I understand." His presence felt as real as a human friend of flesh and blood. His words pierced my heart, and I knew He really knew, felt, and understood my sorrow. I felt deeply understood.

From that time forth, I began experiencing His real, living presence with me every time I walked. He would explain the Scriptures to me in a new way and opened my mind to understanding how He lived the abiding life when He lived on earth and that He had given me the ability to have that same life in Him and the Father. I experienced what is recorded in Luke 24:13–40, in which two of Jesus' disciples walked with Him on the Road to Emmaus. I began a whole new journey with Him in which I really experienced Him with and in me, and that He was not just my Savior who was this historical figure from the Bible. I suddenly experienced, in all its fullness, "the JOY of our salvation." I began understanding more fully what He had accomplished through His death and resurrection, the great power and victory I had over sin through Him. And in addition, I also realized I had never heard this wonderful truth preached in the churches we had attended in my thirty years of Christianity. He began giving me the courage and opportunity to teach others (as He is doing now through this book).

I often find much comfort and encouragement by Oswald Chambers' writings, since he has the ability to affirm what I experience in my walk with Jesus. This devotional, once again, had that effect, since at times I feel like a misfit, even amongst my fellow Christians. Here is what Oswald said that so accurately describes my own experience.

> "After that, He appeared in another form to two of them…" — Mark 16:12 (this is after Jesus resurrection).
>
> Being saved and seeing Jesus are not the same thing. Many people who have never seen Jesus have received and share in God's grace. But once you have seen Him, you can never be the same. Other things will not have the appeal they did before.
>
> You should always recognize the difference between what you see Jesus to be and what He has done for you. If you see only what He has done for you, your God is not big enough. But if you have had a vision, seeing Jesus as He really is, experiences can come and go, yet you will endure "as seeing Him who is invisible" (Hebrews 11:27). The man who was blind from birth did not know who Jesus was until Christ appeared and revealed Himself to him (see John 9).

> Jesus appears to those for whom He has done something, but we cannot order or predict when He will come. He may appear suddenly, at any turn. Then you can exclaim, "Now I see Him!" (see John 9:25).
>
> Jesus must appear to you and to your friend individually; no one can see Jesus with your eyes. And division takes place when one has seen Him and the other has not. You cannot bring your friend to the point of seeing; God must do it. Have you seen Jesus? If so, you will want others to see Him too. 'And they went and told it to the rest, but they did not believe them either' (Mark 16:13). When you see Him, you must tell, even if they don't believe.[2]

I had always heard about the indwelling Holy Spirit, but I felt so disconnected from this Spirit; I felt I couldn't understand or relate to a Spirit being. I could, however, relate to the One who walked this earth as a human, whose name was Jesus.

Understanding the difference between God the Father, the Holy Spirit, and Jesus has caused many confusion. The trinity is such a complex mystery that we may never fully wrap our heads around it. Following is the best way I have come to understand it. Father, Son, and Holy Spirit, are all three spirit, eternal, and have existed from the beginning. All three are persons and were present when the earth was formed—this is where the concept and word Trinity comes from, although it is not a word found in the Scriptures. The Holy Spirit in the Old and New Testaments is the teacher, counselor, power, and communicator between God and man. In the Old Testament, He was not *indwelling, but came upon people* as God the Father, determined and enabled the prophets, who were God's spokespersons, to speak and perform miracles, to reveal His truth, and to convict those who had turned from Him. 2 Peter 1:20–21 states this truth most clearly: *"Above all, you must understand that no prophecy of Scripture came about by the prophet's own interpretation. For prophecy never had its origin in the will of man, but men spoke from God as they were carried along by the Holy Spirit."*

Jesus, as God's Son, was given that name when He entered this world in human form, emptied Himself of all His Godly power and glory (Philippians 2) and relied on the Holy Spirit (as we now do) while ministering on this earth. His role was to show us the Father, so we too could know Him the way He did, to teach us about the Kingdom of God and the abiding life, and then to save us from the bondage/slavery of sin and death through His death and resurrection.

The Holy Spirit, as we know Him in New Testament, was sent by the Father to indwell all who accept Jesus as Christ, the Savior, who took upon Himself our sin by dying on the cross, and resurrected to new life. Together all believers are called the "body of Christ"—the church—to accomplish the same works Jesus did. These are Jesus' own words in John 14:16–17, 25 are: *"'I will ask the Father, and He* *will give you **another Counselor** (emphasis added) to be with you forever—the Spirit of truth. The world cannot accept him, because it neither sees him nor knows him. But you know him, **for he lives with you and will be in you** (emphasis added). All this I have spoken while still with you. But the Counselor (Comforter), the Holy Spirit, whom the Father will send in my name, will teach you all things and will remind you of everything I have said to you'"*. The word *another* in the Greek is—"else, i.e. different (in many applications):—more, one (another), other (wise)." In essence the Holy Spirit who indwells us is one who has the same nature as Jesus and the Father but is different from Jesus who walked in the flesh. The Holy Spirit can do "more" since He indwells all believers, not just Jesus. That is why Jesus made this statement to His disciples: *'"Believe me when I say that I am in the Father and the Father is in me;...I tell you the truth, anyone who has faith in me will do what I have been doing. He will do even greater things than these, because I am going to the Father.'"* (John 14:11–12)

For me, since the indwelling Holy Spirit is the spirit form/version of Jesus, it is most helpful to think of Jesus as the one who is with and in me. Others prefer connecting with the Holy Spirit or the Father/God. However, the matter of greatest importance is the truth that Jesus' presence has taken up residence (dwells, remains, abides) in us, and is the power enabling us to live the resurrection life of Christ.

There is a critical difference in believing whether Jesus is indwelling us or that He is just an historical, external model. The difference is either **imitating or integrating Christ's life—human effort or divine power.**

Oswald describes these thoughts in a powerful way:

> Our Lord's Cross is the gateway into His life... When I was born again, I received the very life of the risen Lord from Jesus Himself... And what His resurrection means for us is that we are raised to His risen life, not to our old life... we can know here and now the power and effectiveness of His resurrection and can "walk in newness of life" (Romans 6:4). The Holy Spirit is the deity of God who... can work the very nature of Jesus into us, if we will only obey Him...[3]

> **"Co-Resurrection...** The Spirit of Jesus entering me rearranges my personal life before God... The Holy Spirit cannot be accepted as a guest in merely one room of the house—He invades all of it. And once I decide that my "old man" (that is, my heredity of sin) should be identified with the death of Jesus, the Holy Spirit invades me. He takes charge of everything. My part is to walk in the light and to obey all that He reveals to me... . God puts the holiness of His Son into me, and I belong to a new spiritual order." This is, what is referred to as, the great exchange. He took my

sinful, old, dead nature into Himself on the cross, and gave me His righteous, holy nature in resurrection."[4]

"Co-Eternal Life... Eternal life is not a gift from God; eternal life is the gift *of God.* 'You shall receive power when the Holy Spirit has come upon you... ' (Acts 1:8)—not power as a gift from the Holy Spirit; the power is the Holy Spirit, not something that He gives us... But once we do decide, the full life of God comes in immediately. Jesus came to give us an endless supply of life—"... that you may be filled with all the fullness of God" (Ephesians 3:19). Eternal life has nothing to do with time. It is the life which Jesus lived when He was down here, and the only Source of life is the Lord Jesus Christ.[5]

"Faith never knows where it is being led, but it loves and knows the One Who is leading." [6]

This life is difficult. Jesus knows that all too well, which is why He is with and in us to live His life in us. We don't have to do it on our own, in our own strength or wisdom; we don't have to try to figure it out to get it right. He has done all of that already for us. We often repeat the Scripture, *"I can do all things through Christ who gives me strength."* But do we really mean it when we continually try to live the Christian life by imitating Him and doing it in our own strength?

This is how Jim May expresses it in his book, *Living at His Place:* "I used to think the Christian life was trying to act like Jesus Christ. But the harder I tried, the more I failed. I could not seem to change myself. Then I saw it! Christianity is not another self-help religion. The goal is not to 'act' like Jesus, but to let Jesus be Himself in me."[7] Can you relate?

These truths are described by Jesus as *"abiding in the vine,"* presented in John 15, to be discussed in future chapter. To put it in my words, when we try to be *like Jesus* we are using our own efforts and **imitating Him;** whereas, if we are totally surrendered to Him who is in us, then we live an **integrated life in Him**. When Jesus cried, *"It is finished"* on the cross, He meant the battle against sin and death is over and won. Now we just need to acknowledge and surrender to His finished work. This is true *rest*, and what the book of Hebrews is all about. I encourage you to read Hebrews, in which we are told that we are now *"at rest and ceased from our labor."* Oh how hard it is to stop striving, to be at rest, and to really walk in that truth.

CHAPTER 7
DO WE IMITATE OR INTEGRATE THE LIFE OF CHRIST?

Many of us, especially if we grew up in church, have frequently heard that we are to *be like Jesus*. We are given examples from the Bible of how Jesus lived and acted, and spoke. We are told that He is our model, teacher, and example whom we are to *imitate.* Years ago the popular thing was to wear a bracelet, which said, "WWJD," meaning "What Would Jesus Do?" So we would make every effort to be like Jesus, using every ounce of our will power and energy, and praying for the Spirit's help in doing so to be more spiritual. Can you relate?

The expressions above sound very spiritual and in some ways like truth, but do they accurately represent what the New Testament teaches? Having said that, I want to be clear that any effort to be like Jesus honors Him and our heavenly Father and adds blessing and joy to our lives. My desire in writing this chapter is to provide my understanding of the difference between the two concepts of *imitating vs. integrating Jesus* by giving the Scriptural principles and explaining some of the pitfalls in the concept of the one versus the other—pitfalls I myself have fallen into and struggled with.

These two terms and concepts may sound very confusing, so I hope you hang in there with me while I try to dig deeper to explain the difference between the two. Before I get into this discussion I want to share some basic facts about the two terms. Both these two words—*integrate* and *imitate*—are not seen in Scripture (just like the word *Trinity* is not); however, the concept of integrating Christ's life into our lives is expressed throughout the New Testament. The word *imitate* is not found in the original Hebrew or Greek, but is only used by the NIV translation in the following verse written by St. Paul to the Corinthian church (I Cor. 4:16): *"Therefore I urge you to imitate me."* The KJV uses the words: *be followers of me*, which is closer to the Greek and is not the same as to *imitate*. Paul expresses the thoughts of *following his example* several times to encourage the newly formed church in being good Christians. He was a human like us, a model, teacher, preacher, and evangelist, who appropriately told his audience, to imitate him.

The term *follow* is also frequently used by Jesus; however, its Greek meaning is "(as a particle of union) and to be in the same way with, i.e., to accompany (spec. as a disciple)." This is a very different meaning from the word *imitate*, and as you will see later, much closer to the concept of the word, *integrate*. There is one account in which Jesus tells His disciples to follow His example—John 13:15—where He washes their feet and instructs them to be servants as He came to serve. However, this was a specific act given as an example, not a process of spiritual growth. I don't recall any other Scripture in which Jesus used the concept of following Him with the understanding of *imitating* Him. Instead, as I will explain shortly, He made it abundantly clear that He would provide a totally new and different way of *following Him and becoming like Him*—the Helper, the Counselor, the Holy Spirit, who would indwell His disciples.

This is how Oswald Chambers expresses similar thoughts:

> "I have been crucified with Christ…"—Galatians 2:20
>
> … Paul said, "I have been crucified with Christ…" He did not say, "I have made a determination to imitate Jesus Christ," or, "I will really make an effort to follow Him"—but—"I have been *identified* with Him in His death."… My unrestrained commitment of myself to God gives the Holy Spirit the opportunity to grant to me the holiness of Jesus Christ.
>
> "… it is no longer I who live…" My individuality remains, but my primary motivation for living and the nature that rules me are radically changed. I have the same human body, but the old satanic right to myself has been destroyed.

"... and the life which I now live in the flesh," not the life which I long to live or even pray that I live, but the life I now live in my mortal flesh—the life which others can see, "I live by faith in the Son of God..." This faith was not Paul's own faith in Jesus Christ, but the faith the Son God had given to him (see Ephesians 2:8). It is no longer a faith in faith, but a faith that transcends all imaginable limits—a faith that comes only from the Son of God."[1]

Now let's read Jesus' own words in John 14:16, in which He teaches His disciples about the Holy Spirit and the integration process of becoming one with/in Him:

*And I will ask the Father, and He will give you another Counselor to be with you forever—the Spirit of truth... you know him, for **he lives with you and will be in you**" John 17:20–28. "'My prayer is not for them alone. I pray also for those who will believe in me through their message, that all of them may be one, Father, just as You **are in Me and I am in You**. May they also be **in us**... I made You known to them, and will continue to make You known in order that the love You have for Me may be in them and that **I Myself may be in them*** (emphasis added).

Jesus' words make it clear that He and His Spirit are the same spirit given to the disciples/us, so that we are *"in Him and He and the Father are in us."* The two separate entities become one. So let's see if we can wrap our minds around this mystery of being *in Him* as spoken by Him.

What Jesus described in the above verses provides an accurate definition of the word to *integrate*—"to make into a whole by bringing all parts together; unify; to join with something else: unite; to make part of a larger unit; to make whole, complete."[2] So then, when the Scripture tells us that we are *"in Christ" and He "is in us,"* we are given a word picture to help us, His disciples, understand that we were two separate entities, which have become one. St Paul in Ephesians 2:12–16 expresses these thought this way:

> *"Remember that at that time you were separate from Christ,... But now in Christ Jesus you who once were far away have been brought near through the blood of Christ. For He Himself is our peace, who has made the two one and has destroyed the barrier, the dividing wall of hostility,... His purpose was to create in Himself one new man out the two, thus making peace, and in this one body to reconcile both of them to God through the cross."*

Now, in reading this passage in its context, I recognize that Paul is talking about the separation between Jews and the Gentiles; however, the principle of becoming "one" with/in Christ is the same, and spoken of throughout the New Testament.

The phrases *"in Him," "in Christ,"* or *"in Jesus,"* are repeated 163 times in the New Testament. That means it is an incredibly important truth, which we need to fully grasp if we are to experience the full benefit of what Christ has and is doing in our lives today, and to experience the joy of our salvation. Following are some of the "in Him" passages. In Romans 6:5 we read:

> *"If we died with Christ, we believe that we will also live with him"; Colossians 2:9–10, 12 — "For in Christ all the fullness of the Deity lives in bodily form, and you haven been given fullness in Christ,... having been buried with Him in baptism and raised with Him through your faith in the power of God, who raised Him from the dead."; 3:4 — "For you died, and your life is now hidden with Christ in God. When Christ, who is your life, appears, then you also will appear with Him in glory; Galatians 3:26–27 — "You are all sons of God through faith in Christ Jesus, for all of you who were baptized into Christ have clothed yourselves with Christ."*

ABIDING

Some of these *"in Christ"* passages also use the word *baptism* as a description/analogy of being *"in Christ"* and a way to help us understand the concept of being integrated into Him.

Here, it is important to correctly understand what the words *baptized* or *baptism* mean. It is not only the act of being baptized with water (as an infant or adult), but also a symbol describing a process. The Greek word means "to *make whelmed, i.e., cover wholly* with a fluid." I Peter 3:18–21 gives us the complete understanding—

> *"For Christ died for sins once for all, the righteous for the unrighteous, to bring you to God. He was put to death in the body but made alive by the Spirit, through whom also He went and preached to the spirits in prison who disobeyed long ago when God waited patiently in the days of Noah while the ark was being built. In it only a few people, eight in all, were saved through water, and this water symbolizes baptism that now saves you also—**not the removal of dirt from the body but the pledge of a good conscience toward God***" (emphasis added).

Another example of baptism is in Luke 12:50, where Jesus using it as a metaphor, rather than the act of baptism— *"'I have come to bring fire on the earth, and how I wish it were already kindled! But I have a baptism to undergo, and how distressed I am until it is completed!'"* These verses define the symbolic process, as an experience that consumes or *overwhelms* or *"make whelmed"* the individual in their relationship to God.

God gave me a way of demonstrating the metaphor of baptism to better understand this truth. I have shared this as a demonstration in a women's Bible study, which seemed helpful to them, so I pray sharing it with you will do likewise. As I walk you through the demonstration, you may want to do this yourself to get the full picture. I suggest you do this in a sink or on a tray.

A Demonstration Symbolizing Baptism in Christ

Take a very large, clear glass vase or container. Fill it with water—symbolizing God the Father, who is Spirit. Take another, smaller clear glass container, representing Jesus the Son, and gently drop it into the larger container—you will note that it will totally fill with water. Then take a very small clear glass container/vase, which you have covered with a filthy dark rag or dead leaf—symbolizing us in our separated, dead, sinful state before Christ. Let the covered container slip out from under the cover (sin)—gently drop it into the middle sized, water-filled, container—representing us who have received Christ. It will also be filled with water. You will notice that each water-filled container is a separate container, yet each is totally filled with the water (symbolizing the Holy Spirit) and can be seen as one whole unit. Going back to our Greek word, as believers in Christ, we are **whelmed, covered, and** one with God's Spirit—Christ, the Father, His disciples (us) are all one and "in" one another

So why did I go to such length to write about integrating Christ's life and being in Christ? What would be the problem with just believing that Jesus is my Savior who is a historical model and teacher to *imitate*? Let's define *imitate*—"to use or follow as a model; **to copy the actions appearance, mannerisms, or speech of; mimic** (emphasis added); to appear like, resemble." [3] From this definition you can see that the meaning and concept of *imitating* is very different from our previous discussion and definition of *integrating*.

There are several pitfalls that can affect our spiritual growth and joy in embracing the process of imitating Jesus rather than integrating Him. First, by imitating Him we rely on our own human effort and we become weary, exhausted, and discouraged, and can easily lose faith and trust in God. This is what I often experienced, and sense others do too. Second if Jesus is seen only as a model to imitate, then we negate the incredible power of the indwelling Holy Spirit, which was gifted to us by Him. In addition, we dismiss all of the New Testament truths, including much of St. Paul's writings, in which he constantly is using the words, in Christ, discussed earlier. Third, we are susceptible to pride as seen in the verse below.

Christ came to *give us Himself in the form of His Spirit, to be integrated* into our lives and to enable us to live a life which glorifies and pleases our heavenly Father, as He did when He walked this earth? Here is how Ephesians 2:8 states this truth: *"For it is by* *grace you have been saved, through faith—and this not from yourselves, it is the **gift of God**—not by works, so that no one can boast* (emphasis added)." Note: our salvation is by grace, not works; and it is **a gift of God Himself, not merely a gift from God**. Why? So none of us can boast.

As usual, the author who best describes and affirms these truths is Oswald Chambers.

> The mystery of sanctification is that the perfect qualities of Jesus Christ are imparted as a gift to me, not gradually, but instantly once I enter by faith into the realization that He "became for [me]... sanctification..." Sanctification means nothing less than the holiness of Jesus becoming mine and being exhibited in my life.
>
> The most wonderful secret of living a holy life does not lie in imitating Jesus, but in letting the perfect qualities of Jesus exhibit themselves in my human flesh. Sanctification is "Christ in you..." (Colossians 1:27). It is *His* wonderful life that is imparted to me in sanctification—imparted by faith as a sovereign gift of God's grace... It is the gift of His patience, love, holiness, faith, purity, and godliness that is exhibited in and through every sanctified soul. Sanctification

is not drawing from Jesus the power to be holy—it is drawing from Jesus the very holiness that was exhibited in Him, and that He now exhibits in me. Sanctification is an impartation, not an imitation. Imitation is something altogether different. The perfection of everything is in Jesus Christ, and the mystery of sanctification is that all the perfect qualities of Jesus are at my disposal. Consequently, I slowly but surely begin to live a life of inexpressible order, soundness, and holiness—"... kept by the power of God..."(1 Peter 1:5).[4]

Scripture makes it abundantly clear that, by faith and acceptance of Christ's death and resurrection, we are made *one with Him*. He is in us and we are in Him, and we have His indwelling power through whom we are capable of living the *abiding life*. More about the term **abiding** will be discussed in the next chapter.

If you are still struggling to wrap your heart and mind around this amazing truth, then this last analogy might help. A while back, when I was trying to teach the role of the Holy Spirit in our lives, Jesus provided this analogy to explain the gift of the Holy Spirit as the process of integrating Christ into our lives. In this analogy, our body is like a car—beautiful, perfectly constructed, mechanically well-fitted. It has everything it needs to function perfectly. It is given as a gift. Everything is done to learn how to drive it and operate it smoothly and safely. You learned by listening to and imitating your instructor(s). Then you take control of the wheel, turn the key; it starts, but quickly stalls after a short drive. You know you have a long distant to go to get to your destination. You see other cars zooming by and feel frustrated, and even begin getting angry, thinking that you were tricked and cheated by the giver of this gift. Finally, you get out and try pushing it or jump-starting it, hoping you can make some progress. Before long you are exhausted and even more discouraged and frustrated. You ask a few passers-by to help you push. They gladly help. Then one of them asks you, "Did you put gas into the car?" With surprise, you answer, "No." After the gas has been gifted (this is where the analogy breaks down, since we receive the Spirit/gas when we receive Christ), miracle of miracles, you get to have complete joy, pleasure, and peace of mind as you drive to your destination with ease and rest. Well, hope you got the picture. Many of us try to do the life of Christ (drive the gifted car) in our own strength, and neglect to rely on the one and only thing to grant success (gas/the Holy Spirit). Do you wonder why you and many of our fellow travelers are burned out, discouraged, and joyless?

In summary, if we don't recognize the truth of Christ in us and only see Him as an historical person and teacher to imitate, we will quickly burn out trying to *be like Christ*. We will get frustrated and discouraged with the little changes in our lives. In our frustration, we may ask God for His strength, peace, patience, love, and so on and wonder why we don't exhibit His attributes. We are asking amiss, because He has already given us absolutely everything we need in Jesus Christ. This is how 2 Peter 1:3–4 states this truth:

> **" His divine power has given us everything we need for life and godliness through our knowledge of Him who called us by His own glory and goodness** (emphasis added*). Through these He has given us His very great and precious promises, so that through them you may participate in the divine nature and escape the corruption in the world caused by evil desires."*

Even though, we have been given this amazing gift, we live as paupers. The problem isn't that we don't have it, but that we haven't had our minds renewed to recognize and surrendered to the One who indwells us, fills us, empowers us, completes us, and enables us to live like Him. To put it crudely—the refrigerator is stocked full and ours for the taking, but we just sit there and ask, "Can you please give me this or that"? In this condition, we are robbed of so much of the joy and abundant fruit of His salvation."

So let's join St Paul in praying these words written in Ephesians 1:7—22:

> *"I keep asking that the God of our Lord Jesus Christ, the glorious Father, may give you/me the Spirit of wisdom and revelation, so that you /I may know Him*

better. I pray also that the eyes of your/my heart may be enlightened in order that you/I may know the hope to which He has called you, the riches of His glorious inheritance in the saints, and His incomparably great power for us who believe. That power is like the working of His mighty strength, which he exerted in Christ when He raised Him from the dead and seated Him at His right hand in the heavenly realms,... And God placed all things under His feet and appointed Him to be head over everything for the church, which is His body, the fullness of Him who fills everything in every way."

Jesus describes these same truths, of the *life in Him*, in John 15 by using another analogy— *"the Vine and the Branches."* This truth, which is recorded by the apostle John, *is* defined as the *abiding* (KJV) *life*. Understanding this Biblical truth has given me the true joy Jesus talked about and told His disciples and us that we could have.

CHAPTER 8
UNDERSTANDING THE **ABIDING LIFE**

John 15:1–17

The word abide is used in the King James Version (KJV), and not commonly used these days, yet its meaning is throughout Scripture and seen in the life Jesus when he walked this earth. The Greek definition of abiding is—"a prim. verb; to stay (in a given place, state, relation or expectancy):—continue, dwell, endure, be present, remain, stand, tarry (for), thine (His) own." The clearest picture of abiding has been given to us by Jesus, as recorded in John 15:1–17—the vine and the branches, which was the Scripture God used to deepen my understanding of the personal relationship with Him, and profoundly impacted my spiritual growth and walk.

Since Christ opened my understanding of the abiding life, I have often struggled to wrap my head around what it really looks like, how to explain it, what it really means, and how to walk it out in my own life. I have wrestled with questions such as, When am I abiding? Does abiding/remaining mean that I have to consciously think about Him 100 percent of the time? If I sin, does it mean that I have stopped abiding? Am I only abiding when I am bearing fruit, and what is meant by bearing fruit? Before I share some of the ways He answered these questions let's review Jesus' words:

> *"I am the true vine, and my Father is the gardener... Remain (abide, KJV) in me and I will remain in you. No branch can bear fruit by itself; it must remain in the vine. Neither can you bear fruit unless you remain in me. I am the vine; you are the branches. If a man remains in me and I in him;, he will bear much fruit; apart from me you can do nothing.... This is to my Father's glory, that you bear much fruit, showing yourselves to be my disciples. As the Father has loved me, so have I loved you. Now remain in my love. If you obey my commands, you will remain in my love; just as I have obeyed my Father's commands and remain in his love. I have told you this so that my joy may be in you and that your joy may be complete."*

It is obvious from these verses, that the disciples' life (the branches) is intimately connected and surrendered to Christ (the vine). It is the *integrated life* of which I spoke earlier. It is **not**, as we often think, me living my life and asking Him to be part of it at my request. It also is **not** being 100 percent consciously focused on Him.

ABIDING

I often thought abiding meant I had to think about spiritual things (Jesus) all the time. So, needless to say, I felt frustrated and like I was failing Jesus and my heavenly Father, since none of us can be focused on spiritual matters all day and night. It was after I received these analogies that I was able to live in peace and rest.

The first analogy has come from my walks on the beach, both in California and in my current time in South Padre Island. In the first analogy the ocean is like God—vast, immeasurable, His depth inconceivable, constantly moving, powerful, and full of life. The ocean doesn't disappear just because I am not walking on its shores. It is my choice and conscious decision whether I *draw near* or not, whether I choose to experience it. Similarly, God is present whether I am walking in conscious awareness of Him or not; however, in both cases, I only fully experience the blessings and benefits when I draw near and focus on them. Because we are finite creatures who (for most of us do not live as monks) have to live a temporal life in this world, we cannot and are not capable of focusing our attention on God and Spiritual matters all day and night. But does it mean, that when I am not focusing on God, that I am not abiding? No. This is the truth that helped set me free from guilt and confusion. I am God's child, Jesus' sister, and a branch in the vine as long as I am not choosing to reject Christ, the vine. Jesus told us that He holds us in the palm of His hands and no one can take us out (John 10:28, 29).

The second analogy is one you may more easily relate to, and that is our most intimate relationships on earth. I spoke in an earlier chapter about this. The healthiest, most intimate relationships are those in which we consciously make time to communicate deeply—sharing our hearts and listening to understand one another, loving and accepting one another unconditionally, honoring each other and supporting one another according to our needs. However, it is impossible to communicate with each other on a deep level 100 percent of the time. Whether we are married or a parent with children or living with a close friend/sister and share a home we are not physically/consciously together all the time. It is a fluent state of relating, which fluctuates between intense moments of deep, focused attention and/or simply being in the home together without a word or physical contact. Does it mean that when we are not in the same space with one another or having deep, intimate conversations, that we are no longer married, parent, sibling, or friend? The obvious answer is, **no**. Likewise, we *"abide/remain"* in Christ and are part of His household (John 14), are a branch in the vine, and are part of the bride of Christ (the church) as long as we don't sever or walk away, divorce ourselves from Him. Looking back at the definition of *abiding*, this is precisely what it says, *"to stay (in a given place, state, relation or expectancy):—continue, dwell, endure, be present*, remain, stand, tarry (for), thine (KJV) own."

In one of my recent walks on the beach, Jesus spoke and helped me to see another beautiful example of this abiding experience. I had been doing a lot of writing and felt overwhelmed with all I had received. So when I started our walk I asked Jesus if we could just

ABIDING

walk and not focus on anything deep or serious. I heard Him chuckle and say to me, "I just want to have fun too." His use of the word *fun* took me back for a moment, but I felt myself relax and just enjoy the scenery with Him. I observed the multitude of seashells and heard Him remind me that He has created each to be unique and special, just like the individuality of people. We gazed at the vast hues of the gulf waters and enjoyed the balmy breeze and warmth of the sun. Then He drew my attention to several couples or dads with toddlers. They would be holding hands, huddled in embrace, or carried on the dad's shoulder. There was such joy and pure pleasure expressed on their faces as they enjoyed each other. As I took in these scenes, I saw my heavenly Father smile and say, "See the joy in their faces? That is the same joy I feel when we are in each other's presence. That is all I want of you and my children—to hold your hand or carry you on my shoulder. That simple trust is all I desire and gives me such joy." And I felt His joy and lightness of heart and spirit.

Then, Jesus spoke, giving me the words He spoke to His disciples as recorded in John 4:34; *"My food… is to do the will of him who sent me, and to finish his work."* I was puzzled by His statement, but He continued. "I didn't say My food is to make a five-year plan, or build a church, or save so many souls, or preach and teach to so many people, or feed and care for the needy, or reach out to love your neighbor, or run this and that ministry at the church, or pray for and heal this or that person. My eyes were always, only on and My Father." His point was, His focus was only on His Father, who had sent Him. His one and only mission, was to please the Father by living a surrendered, dependent, *abiding,* obedient life. And as He did that, the Father empowered Him do and accomplish all these other things, but the ministry wasn't the focus. Jesus spoke these words to His disciples: *"For I did not speak of my own accord, but the Father who sent me commanded me what to say and how to say it…. So whatever I say is just what the Father has told me to say."*

This is how Oswald Chambers states this truth:

> The Spirit of Jesus is conscious of only one thing—a perfect oneness with the Father. And He tells us, "Take My yoke upon you and learn from Me, for I am gentle and lowly in heart, and you will find rest for your souls" (Matthew 11:29). All I do should be based on a perfect oneness with Him, not on a self-willed determination to be godly. There is no condition of life in which we cannot abide in Jesus. We have to learn to abide in Him wherever we are placed[1]

You see, where we miss the joy and the power and get burned out in ministry is when we focus on the success of the product—the what, where, how, when, and to whom. We take Jesus' commands and read about His life and then wear ourselves out and get tied up in knots trying to accomplish what He did. We try so hard to be like, look like, sound like, pray like, and live like Jesus, but our focus is

ABIDING

on the ministry goal, and the end product/result, rather than on Him. Then we wonder why we have no real joy or peace or patience, or kindness, and feel more often like a big zero in the eyes of God rather than a victorious Christian. We wonder where the joy, the fruit, and freedom that we are promised in the Scriptures?

To summarize, we are abiding in Christ, whether we are consciously aware and present to Him or not. Abiding is not dependent upon our conscious awareness of Jesus, but **a state of being that He has established** with our agreement/surrender to Him. And the joy of His salvation is because of this gift of connectedness with Him. It is not earned nor maintained by my efforts. Let's go back to the definition given earlier of abiding—"to stay (*in a given place, state, relation or expectancy); continue, dwell,* endure, be present, stand, tarry." Note, it is a *given relationship* by God through faith in Christ, not one earned by our actions. However, whether I will benefit from that relationship, or bear fruit, or have fullness of joy totally depends on how deeply I am drawing near and staying connected. I will bear much fruit and experience far more blessing of the abundant life promised if I spend conscious, focused time with Him, like marriage, parenthood, and friendship, and walking on the beach, enjoying the wonders of life.

Now I'd like to answer the question about, whether I stop abiding when I sin. To answer this we can also use the marriage/intimate relationship. There is not one relationship on earth in which we don't grieve each other by sinning. However, saying or doing something that offends or hurts our loved one doesn't mean that it ends the relationship. It will temporarily cause a rift and tension, but it won't bring about a divorce. Likewise, we belong to Christ and are in Him even when we grieve Him by our sin. Sinning may cause some obstruction between us and God, like blockage in the pathways of the branches or like built up cholesterol in our veins, which hinder the effective witness of Christ. He desires to clear out those hindrances (hence the work of the Holy Spirit to convict us of sin), but that does not sever our connection with Him. If sin exists we may not bear as much fruit; consequently not glorifying God. There is need to acknowledge the sin and ask forgiveness in order to feel that closeness and unity and fulfill God's purpose in us.

During the time in which I was caring for my mother (my sweet, gentle, quiet-spirited mama), I became painfully aware of how little of the fruit of the Spirit I had and how miserably I was failing as a daughter and a Christian. I tried to be spiritual and show patience, kindness, love, joy, and peace towards her. I would pray for patience and love. Then Jesus taught me another huge truth of abiding—how the fruit of the Spirit is produced in our lives. The guilt and shame was replaced by joy and freedom. You may also be struggling, as I did, and often pray for more patience, peace, or kindness. So I would like to share these truths, with the prayer that you too may find new joy and freedom.

CHAPTER 9
HOW THE FRUIT OF THE SPIRIT IS PRODUCED IN OUR LIVES

John 15:18-21

We just explored the John 15 verses, in which Jesus talked about the abiding life and how our heavenly Father is glorified and has joy when we produce fruit. However, it seems to me that there is much confusion and misunderstanding on the subject of bearing fruit and different interpretations of what "fruit" is. Yet, Jesus made it clear that our ability to have joy is connected with producing fruit. (You may want to re-read the John 15 verses in the previous chapter). One of the misinterpretations of bearing fruit of which I have heard (and thought) is that it is what we produce for Christ. For example: witnessing and bringing someone to Christ or teaching/preaching and seeing lives changed for Christ. These are what I would refer to as the harvest rather than the fruit. So let's see if we can get some clarity on this subject.

HOW THE FRUIT OF THE SPIRIT IS PRODUCED IN OUR LIVES

In addition to the verses in John 15, fruit is also listed in Galatians 5:25. The Greek word for *fruit* in Galatians 5:22-23, John 15, and Revelations 22:2 is the same. The Scripture in Galatians 5:22-23 is as follows: *"The fruit of the Spirit is love, joy, peace, patience, kindness, goodness, faithfulness, gentleness and self-control."* Think about Christ's nature; is He not described with these same characteristics?

Frequently, I hear people pray (and have prayed myself) for peace, patience, kindness, or to be more loving—as stated above, the fruit of the Spirit. The way growth of the fruit in our lives has been taught is that we gradually grow the fruit as we mature in Christ. In other words, my personality or character slowly becomes more patient, loving, kind, and/or joyful. Since fruit (in nature) develops slowly over time when a tree is well watered and given all the necessary ingredients, a parallel process is assumed to develop the spiritual fruit in our lives. It made a lot of sense, so I would try very hard to read the Bible, pray, and go to church to provide the right conditions in order to become more like Christ. And yet, it seemed I always fell short of being as loving, joyful, peaceful, patient, kind, good, faithful, self-controlled, and so on as I thought Christ would be, and as I ought to be. Can you relate?

Another frustration I encountered in trying to grow the Spiritual fruit is that at some moments in my life I did pretty well, but then the next day or even next hour I would be back to exhibiting the works of the flesh (2 Cor. 12:20). There was no consistency, no permanence. If growing fruit gradually, as believed above, would develop those characteristics or traits in my life, then why weren't they a stable component of my maturing character in Christ? The definition of *character trait* is "the pattern of collective character, behavioral, temperamental, emotional, and mental traits of a person," and trait "a genetically determined characteristic or condition."[1] From one of my early psychology classes, I recall that character traits were a stable part of our human personality. If that is true, then why wasn't my effort in developing those Christ-like characteristics consistent in my life?

Reading John 15 and talking and listening to God helped me to understand how the fruit of the Spirit is produced in our lives. First, of note, is that the *fruit* is singular, not fruits, plural—one source with many attributes. The **only way** fruit is evident (not developed gradually) is by abiding, remaining attached securely and completely to Him. As His (the vine's) essence flows through and into us (the branches), the branches' nature will emulate that of the vine and the fruit (of the Spirit) will be apparent. Let's look again at select passages of Jesus' own words, as spoken to His disciples in John 15:1 — 17 —

> *"I am the true vine, and my Father is the gardener... Remain (abide) in me and I will remain (abide) in you. No branch can bear fruit by itself; it must remain in the vine. Neither can you bear fruit unless you remain in me. I am the vine; you are the branches. If a man remains in me and I in him; he will bear much fruit;*

apart from me you can do nothing… . This is to My Father's glory, that you bear much fruit, showing yourselves to be my disciples. As the Father has loved me, so have I loved you. Now remain in my love… ***I have told you this so that my joy may be in you and that your joy may be complete…****(emphasis added). I chose you and appointed you to go and bear fruit— fruit that will last."*

It is critical for us to look at the words Jesus used. He told His disciples that if they/we remain (abide) in Him, they *"will bear"* much fruit. He does not say, "might bear," and does not use the words produce or develop fruit. This is a big distinction. In other words, the fruit is the evidence of the action of being *"in Him"*; when I am totally surrendered to Him, and one with Him, the fruit is the evidence. As the verse above stated, the evidence that we are Jesus' disciples is by bearing fruit—we are like Him. Why? Because the *"fruit of the Spirit"* described above is His very nature and character. He is love, joy, peace, patience, and kindness. So when and if I am one with Him (as the branch is to the vine) His very own nature will be evident in and through my behavior and attitude. The big truth is this: ***it never will be my effort or gradual maturation in Him that slowly changes my personality to look like His. It is, and always will be, only His nature in me*** as I am completely surrendered, *abiding* in Him. This is a moment by moment, conscious decision, with the hope that the

ABIDING

longer we walk with Christ we will learn and be more consistently abiding in Him—showing more fruit (His nature) in our lives.

Strong's Concordance Helps Word-Studies says this: "2590 properly fruit; (figuratively) everything done in true partnership with Christ, i.e. a believer (a branch) lives in union with Christ (the vine). By definition, fruit (2590/karpos) results from two life-streams—the Lord living His life through ours—to yield what is eternal."[2] Some additional Scriptures to help us fully understand the above verses are in Galatians 3:2–3, 5, 14 we are told that we "received" the Spirit by faith, not by the law, (works of the flesh). Paul then continues as he challenges us with this question: *"Are you so foolish? Having begun by the Spirit, are you now being perfected by the flesh?"* Then in 5:24–26 St. Paul tells us: *"Now those who belong to Christ Jesus have crucified the flesh with its passions and desires. If we live by the Spirit, let us also walk by the Spirit. Let us not become boastful,..."* All these verses describe a completed result and not a gradual process of becoming, which is totally gained or evidenced in a life surrendered/yielded to Christ. The above verses also point out one of the dangers in trying to use fleshly effort in producing life of the Spirit—*pride*. Pride, as we know, is God's biggest enemy. It is opposed to Christ's nature and, therefore, will rob us of all joy.

I want to share a personal example of this. During the time of writing this book, I was having my quiet time and felt convicted by a devotional that focused on the topic of James 3:5–12, the controlling of the tongue and using it to criticize others. I became aware that I also tend to be critical with a certain person, so I asked God why I was critical. I didn't receive an answer right away, but later, when I was reading in Jim May's book, *Living at His Place*. I knew God was using this writing to answer my question. I had become prideful and taken credit for the spiritual fruit of self-control. I am very conscious of how I spend time, money, and so on. Although, I may have an understanding of the underlying reasons, from a psychological perspective for these behaviors, I have a great distaste for wastefulness of any kind. I tend to be critical of anyone lacking self-control and having addictive behaviors. However, God showed me that this characteristic of self-control really is one of His fruits, and has been part of my life as a result of living in Christ. (On the lighter side, I cannot dismiss some of my Dutch heritage as having an influence as well.) But because I took credit for it as part of my personality trait and Christian maturity, I became prideful, and in that pride I became critical of those who don't exhibit this character. I then further realized that a critical spirit often stems from a spirit of pride. I felt the grief of my Father at that moment and asked His forgiveness.

Over the many years of attending church, I have also seen this critical spirit displayed in other Christians. They become critical of those who don't seem to care about the same concerns in ministry or don't act as loving or patient, or have as much faith, or don't seem as committed to Bible study or prayer, or Scripture memorization. What is really behind that criticism is the thought that they are, and do it,

ABIDING

better, which is pride. Can you see this in your life? Jesus made this point with the following parable in Luke 18:9–14:

> *"Then he gave this illustration to certain people who were confident of their own goodness and looked down on others: "Two men went up to the Temple to pray, one was a Pharisee, the other was a tax-collector. The Pharisee stood and prayed like this with himself, 'O God, I do thank you that I am not like the rest of mankind, greedy, dishonest, impure, or even like that tax-collector over there. I fast twice every week; I give away a tenth-part of all my income.' But the tax collector stood in a distant corner, scarcely daring to look up to Heaven, and with a gesture of despair, said, 'God, have mercy on a sinner like me.' I assure you that he was the man who went home justified in God's sight, rather than the other one. For everyone who sets himself up as somebody will become a nobody, and the man who makes himself nobody will become somebody."* (Phillip's)

This is what St. Paul writes about pride: I Corinthians 4:7 says, "**What do you have that you did not receive? But if you did receive it, why do you boast as if you had not received it.**" Pride is the greatest

HOW THE FRUIT OF THE SPIRIT IS PRODUCED IN OUR LIVES

enemy to the abiding life of Christ; however, there are other negative effects that rob us of joy.

If we recognize that Christ's nature is integrated into our lives by abiding, then we can stop exhausting ourselves by trying to develop Christ's characteristics (fruit), as well as His work in ministry by our own willpower. We don't have to beat ourselves up, when we are not consistent, which causes discouragement and makes us vulnerable to Satan's lie that we are not maturing and growing in Christ. In addition, and most important, we don't have to be subject to Satan's accusations and feel guilt and shame, which are the biggest joy killers.

I believe all of us sincerely do want to obey God, please Him, bear fruit, and show that we love Him. Trying so hard and failing becomes a constant source of frustration, discouragement, and a burden our Father never meant for us to bear. Jesus told us that, *"His burden is light"* (Matthew 11:28). So let's not keep struggling in the flesh and join our brother Jesus in sharing His joy completely (John 15:11). When we recognize we have fallen short of His perfection, we simple confess it and turn back to surrendering to Him who is in me, letting Him be the one who produces, not me. This is allowing God to be God in my life instead of me trying to be god. We then, once again, abide in the freedom and joy that His salvation has given to us as a gift through faith.

Another area of confusion is the topic of spiritual gifts and talents.

ABIDING

What are the Gifts of the Spirit and How Do We Receive Them?

Just like there can be confusion about the fruit of the Spirit, I have seen that there can be difficulty in understanding the *Gifts of the Spirit*, and how they are received. The Gifts of the Spirit are listed in I Corinthians 12–13; Romans 12; and Ephesians 4:11–13. They are accurately named the "***gifts***" of the Spirit because the Holy Spirit gives them to us when we are born again (saved), and are not produced by our own efforts. They are also not those personality traits or genetic dispositions or talents with which we are born in the flesh.

Paul has this to say:

> *"For by the grace given me I say to every one of you: Do not think of yourself more highly than you ought, but rather think of yourself with sober judgment, in accordance with the measure of faith God has given you. Just as each of us has one body with many members, and these members do not all have the same function, so in Christ we who are many form one body, and each member belongs to all the other.* ***We have different gifts, according to the grace given us*** (emphasis added)." (Romans 12:3–6)

As the above passage states, we were given these gifts by God to be *the body of Christ,* doing His work here on earth, and to build up fellow believers. The gifts never were meant for our personal benefit or profit. However, by allowing ourselves to be Christ's vessel through which His gifts flow, we are a blessing and are tremendously blessed as well. Listen to Paul's words given in Ephesians 4:11–14:

> "It was he who gave some to be apostles, some to be prophets, some to be evangelists, and some to be pastors and teachers, to prepare God's people for works of service, so that the body of Christ may be built up, until we all reach unity in the faith and in the knowledge of the Son of God and become mature, attaining to the whole measure of the fullness of Christ… Speaking the truth in love, we will in all things grow up into him who is the Head, that is, Christ. From him the whole body, joined and held together by every supporting ligament, grows and builds itself up in love, as each part does its work."

The feeling I have experienced when I am walking out this truth in my life are as follows: like all is well with my soul, I am whole, I am home. It is the greatest joy and blessing. Oddly enough, that is exactly what Christ said would happen in John 15:11 — *"Now remain in my love…I have told you this so that my joy may be in you and that your joy may be complete…"* He says, *"His joy may be complete."*

We share in His joy. Why? Because we are one with Him. **Amazing**. This joy truly is a gift of our salvation.

In Romans 12:3–6, Paul warns the church of the pitfall and danger caused by having an incorrect understanding of the gifts and their use—that of pride. Just like taking credit for the fruit of the spirit, we can become prideful for the gifts of the Spirit. We can quickly be possessive, competitive, and controlling in the ministry(ies) in which we are involved. On the other hand, if we don't acknowledge or recognize the gifts of the Spirit we have received, we are handicapped in our ministries.

Now that we have explored the reasons and ability to enjoy the wonderful blessings of our salvation in Christ, you may be asking questions such as, "What if I am feeling grief, sadness, frustration, and anger? Does it mean I am not abiding in Christ? Is there something wrong with me? And if I am struggling with trials, am I supposed to feel happy about it? One of the verses, which we often get stumped on, is James 1:2–4. Let's delve into it to help us better understand.

CHAPTER 10

IF I HAVE THE JOY OF GOD'S SALVATION SHOULD I EXPERIENCE GRIEF AND SORROW?

James 1:2-4; John 15:18-21

There are many different teachings in the church on the subject of suffering. Some preach that all suffering is due to sin and Satan's effect on our lives, and Christians ought not to suffer. Another is that, as children of God we live a protected, blessed life and are spared suffering, because we are His beloved. Since Jesus suffered and spoke to His disciples of the suffering they would experience, I have difficulty accepting the above perspectives. So what is the truth on the subject of suffering and trials? And how do we reconcile the subject of this book—joy—and feeling the pain of trials.

Let's take a look at the verse in James 1:2–4: *"My brothers, count it a joy when you fall into various trials,* **knowing that the testing of your faith produces patience**. *But let patience have its perfect work, that you may be perfect and complete, lacking nothing"* (NKJV). We

ABIDING

often struggle with these verses when we only understand them via our English language, consequently interpreting the verse to mean that we are to have joy in and for our trials. Given that interpretation, our response is; "How can our compassionate, heavenly Father tell us to have joy when we face trials or temptations? Joy? I am supposed to have joy?" That makes no sense and doesn't seem loving, and it certainly does not seem realistic. In fairness, if that is the meaning we would be right to feel that way. So again, it will help if we understand these words in the original Greek language.

Let's pull the verse apart and look at their Greek meaning. First, it does not say that we should have joy or rejoice **for** the trial, but for the result or **outcome of the trial.** The KJV uses the word "**produces patience.**" The Greek for *patience* is: "cheerful (or hopeful) endurance, constancy, patient continuance; to stay under, **remain, abide, continue, dwell** (emphasis added)." Haven't we seen those words before? Yes, the goal and the outcome of the trial, as intended by our loving heavenly Father and Jesus, is **to produce the "abiding life and therefore a completeness in Christ Jesus.** That is the reason for joy and not the suffering in the trial. It is a similar concept described in Hebrews 12:1–3, when it says,

> *"Therefore,... let us throw off everything that hinders and the sin that so easily entangles, and let us run with perseverance (patience) the race marked out for us. Let us fix our eyes on Jesus, the author and*

IF I HAVE THE JOY OF GOD'S SALVATION SHOULD I EXPERIENCE GRIEF AND SORROW?

> *perfecter of our faith, who for the joy set before him, endured the cross, scorning its shame, and sat down at the right hand of the throne of God. Consider him, who endured such opposition from sinful men, so that you will not grow weary and lose heart".*

Notice it doesn't say that He had joy in bearing the cross or all its horrendous shame and pain. We also know that He was in deep anguish and pleaded with His Father to have the trial *cup removed*. Yet, He ultimately submitted to His Father's will.

Our Father and Jesus do not expect us to enjoy the trial, but He allows them, knowing that this is the way we get to the ultimate goal of an abiding life and completeness in Christ. It is also of interest that the James 1:1–4 verses are followed by an encouragement for us to ask for wisdom if we lack it (v. 5). We cannot see and understand God's perspective through our human understanding. We absolutely need His wisdom, Word, His heart, and His faith to endure and persevere. Also notice that God *"gives (wisdom) to all men generously and without finding fault."*

Jim May puts it this way:

> Our Father wants us to become as little children so we can enter His kingdom; therefore, He will allow us to be in situations where we are totally helpless… God desires to have children who will let Him be their

Father. But if we rely on ourselves, we will never rely on Him enough and see His wonderful provision and protection... We must get to the end of ourselves to see Him!... We can be sure that the circumstances (trials) are individually designed... Is this cruel on His part? No. Never! He wants us to humble ourselves before Him and be set free.[1]

It is also of great importance to remember that our Father is not up in heaven laughing at us while we suffer, but that He grieves with us the way Jesus wept and grieved with those He loved when they were suffering (John 11:35).

In Luke 6:20–23 Jesus gives, what are best known as the Beatitudes, in which He lists all the *"Blessed are you."* From our human/worldly perspective, each circumstance listed, as *blessed* would be the total opposite of what we view as a blessing (a source of joy). We do everything we can to avoid suffering and trials, and complain bitterly when we do experience these situations. Yet in verse 23 Jesus says, *"Be glad in that day, and leap for joy, for behold, your reward is great in heaven."* Why would it be a blessing? The answer is quite simple. Unless we are needy, unhappy, depleted in strength or emotion, or dissatisfied, we don't tend to depend on God and come to Him. Isn't it true that most of us go about life, and turn to God only when we are in a crisis and hurting, or at the end of our

IF I HAVE THE JOY OF GOD'S SALVATION SHOULD I EXPERIENCE GRIEF AND SORROW?

rope (hopeless/helpless)? That may be why God sovereignly allows these trials into our lives.

This same spirit and experience is described by St. Paul as quoted by Sheridan Voysey, of Our Daily Bread.

> 2 Corinthians 6:3–10 *"Our hearts ache, but we always have joy. We are poor, but we give spiritual riches to others. We own nothing, and yet we have everything…"*

The apostle Paul found the answer. In the midst of being chased, beaten, slandered, and unjustly imprisoned—even when he was hungry, exhausted, and impoverished—he could say that he had "joy" (2 Corinthians 6:5–10). How? Because he knew that with God no pain is wasted (Romans 5:2–5). But even more significantly, his joy was sourced in the Holy Spirit who brings joy no matter the circumstances (Galatians 5:22–23). Happiness is often found in outside circumstances, but real joy flows from the Holy Spirit who lives within us.

So savor today's moments of happiness—the tastes, the conversations, the sunlit valleys. They're good gifts to be enjoyed. But find the fullness of joy in the

> One who can lift and comfort you even in the unhappiest of times. [2]

We can only have the *joy of our salvation* when we see things through the eyes of Christ and live fully one with His Spirit. I believe our heavenly Father desires and has enabled each of His children to fully experience the joy of His salvation and that it is for everyone not just a few select, but how and when we experience the joy becomes a unique, personal experience and journey with Him.

John 15:18-21; 16:20, 33

Next, I want to put our suffering and trials into perspective, by quoting Jesus' own words to His disciples as given in the gospel of John.

> *"If the world hates you, keep in mind that it hated me first... If they persecuted me, they will persecute you also... I tell you the truth, you will weep and mourn while the world rejoices. You will grieve, but your grief will turn to joy... I have told you these things, so that in me you may have peace. In this world you will have trouble. But take heart! I have overcome the world".*

Here again, Jesus is showing empathy for the pain and grief they/we will suffer; however, He makes two important points. First, that they/we shouldn't be surprised when suffering comes, since they/we will experience what He experienced. Second, that they/we can and will have joy and peace, even in the midst of the trial, because of what the end outcome of the suffering will produce—like a woman in childbirth (John 16:21).

A writer in the Dailey Bread Journal wrote this comment:

> I recently watched a viral video in which men were voluntarily subjected to pain similar to what women experience in childbirth. The men began the experiment in good spirits, joking around as electrodes were attached to their abdomens. But as the pain began and eventually increased, they started to grimace and wince in pain—eventually screaming and clutching each other's hands for emotional support. As I watched the video, I thought about my own wife—the mother of our five kids—and couldn't help but wonder: *How do women endure that kind of suffering?*
>
> The answer is that although childbirth may cause intense pain, there's an invaluable point to the pain: a *baby!* It's the baby that allows women to place their experience into a larger context and to realize that,

as painful as childbirth is, it results in the birth of a beautiful new life. In that way, their pain isn't an end unto itself, but a chapter of a larger story.

Although Jesus is fully God, His human suffering on earth was far more profound and severe than what we might face, as evidenced by His night in the garden of Gethsemane (Luke 22:44). What allowed Him to endure suffering of this magnitude was the joy that would come after it: His great victory over sin and death (Hebrews 12:2). Jesus knew that His pain, although indescribable, was only part of the larger story of salvation. And so He was able to endure.

How important it is for us to take the same approach— choosing not to "give up" when we face trials and tribulations (Hebrews 12:3). They aren't the entire story of our lives, but merely a chapter. May we rest in God and His infinite power and love, knowing that He can work through even our deepest pain.[3]

Following are additional examples from Scripture that speak of the reason and ability to have joy in our trials: 1 Peter 1:6—9; 1 Peter 2:21—23; Job 42:5; Romans 8:37 *"In all these things we are more than conquerors through Him who loved us."*

Oswald says the following:

> We are super-victors with a joy that comes from experiencing the very things, which look as if they are going to overwhelm us.
>
> Huge waves that would frighten an ordinary swimmer produce a tremendous thrill for the surfer who has ridden them. Let's apply that to our own circumstances. The things we try to avoid and fight against—tribulation, suffering, and persecution—are the very things that produce abundant joy in us. "We are more than conquerors through Him," "*in* all these things"; not in spite of them, but in the midst of them. A saint doesn't know the joy of the Lord in spite of tribulation, but *because* of it. Paul said, "I am exceedingly joyful in all our tribulation" (2 Corinthians 7:4).
>
> "The undiminished radiance, which is the result of abundant joy, is not built on anything passing, but on the love of God that nothing can change. And the experiences of life, whether they are everyday events or terrifying ones, are powerless to "separate us from the love of God which is in Christ Jesus our Lord" (Romans 8:39).[4]

Christ is always the ultimate example to follow and help us understand the joy in suffering. Hebrews 12:1–3 tells us this: *"Let us fix our eyes on Jesus, the author and perfecter of our faith, who for the joy set before him endured the cross, scorning its shame,… Consider him who endured such opposition from sinful man, so that you will not grow weary and lose heart."*

At this point, some of you may be protesting and thinking, Maria you are not dealing with the reality of life by writing about so much joy and bliss. And you would be right and fair in thinking that. To take it one step further, you may be tempted to put this book down and quit reading, because discouragement and guilt have overcome you. You may be reviewing your own life and thinking, *If I don't have joy then I'm not a Christian or living as a Christian.* In the verses just discussed, Jesus made it clear to His disciples (and us) that He expects and understands that there will be grief and sorrow. In fact He wants you to know He understands, because He makes it clear in Scripture, and also spoke to me and stopped me in writing about joy in the middle of this book, which I will share next.

Lamentations, Crying Out to God, Grief, and Despair in Scripture

If we read the whole Bible, especially the Psalms, we see many of God's chosen and anointed who expressed raw, honest lamenting. They speak for all of us in our suffering and can provide the words we sometimes feel, yet dare not express to God or anyone else. So this

IF I HAVE THE JOY OF GOD'S SALVATION SHOULD I EXPERIENCE GRIEF AND SORROW?

may help us to realize that our Father does not, and will not, reject us if we cry out to Him. As stated in chapter two, He grieves with us. Jesus helped me to see this more clearly when He abruptly changed the subject from joy to sorrow during one of my walks on the beach.

This is what He laid upon my heart to share with you. I was feeling great blessedness and peace for everything I was experiencing—the beauty of the beach, no pressure or demands on my life, receiving all that God was giving me to write, and the relaxing time with my husband—oh, and the good food. But as I was walking, I suddenly felt the joy leave and a spirit of heaviness come upon me. I still felt Christ's Spirit with me, but it was as though He was reminding me about another truth of Who He is— *"a man of sorrow and acquainted with grief"* (Isaiah 53:3). So I stilled my brain and asked Him to speak, and I tried to listen. To be honest, it was difficult; I didn't want to hear or experience this part. But as I held onto Him and His sweet presence, I felt His strength and courage to listen. This is what He spoke to me in His gentle voice.

"Life in Me is not just joy but also sorrow and grief. I am grieved when My disciples don't experience my presence. I am broken-hearted with the brokenness, sickness, and death in My world. I grieve over My creation and the sorrow you bare is My grief and sorrow, and I carry it with you. But the grief will not overwhelm you, and you will be able to endure it, if you draw near to Me and let me carry it with you. Then you will feel My presence, My peace, My strength. This is what I meant when I said, *'My yoke is easy and my burden is light'* "(Matt. 11: 28). As you abide in me, we are carrying the brokenness of this world together."

I then remembered times (not too long ago) that I experienced deep grief, sorrow, pain, and powerlessness, yet absolute trust in my heavenly Father, because of extreme brokenness with one of my own family members. I recall, often feeling the pain and anguish of clients in counseling sessions as they shared their pain of abuse or broken relationships. Jesus then let me know that there will be times in the future when I will again feel this sorrow (although He did not give details as to why, what, or when). I continued to feel the heaviness but with it a strong sense of peace and His presence. Other examples came to mind from Scripture that spoke of Jesus' grief: Luke 19:41–42, when Jesus wept over Jerusalem just before His crucifixion; when He wept at His friend Lazarus' grave (John 11:35).

The following is a quote from an entry in Our Daily Bread.

Philippians 3:17

Several years ago I received a letter from an *Our Daily Bread* reader after I had written about a family tragedy. "When you told about your tragedy," this person wrote, "I realized that the writers were real people with real problems." How true that is! I look across the list of men and women who pen these articles, and I see cancer and wayward children and unfulfilled dreams and many other kinds of loss. We are indeed just regular, real people writing about a real God who understands our real problems.

The apostle Paul stands out in the Real People Hall of Fame. He had physical problems. He had legal issues. He had interpersonal relationship struggles to deal with. And in all of this messy reality, he was setting an example for us.[5]

One additional thought about why we experience trials—God may be using our trials and our response in it as a witness to the unbelievers around us. It may not be at all to sanctify our lives. The book of Job is our best example for this. Job was called a righteous man, yet he suffered unimaginable trials. So our suffering may be for the sole purpose of being a witness of Christ in us in the midst of pain and difficulties. I've heard this question asked: "Why is it that those most committed to God seem to suffer the most?" I have come to believe that God knows what and how His disciples will bear up in trials and be a testimony of Christ's Spirit in the midst of suffering. We are to be set apart (holy) from the world around us, and the unholy response of those still walking in darkness. This is another reason we need to totally rely on Christ's Spirit in us when we are facing trials. We cannot do this if we rely on our own will power or strength.

So, dear brother and sister in Christ, I (or rather Jesus) don't want you to feel shame and guilt if you are struggling with grief, deep sadness, pain, and even despair. Jesus knows and is carrying it with you. Your heavenly Father understands what you are going through. He has great compassion for you and wants you to "come to Him" with your sorrows in honesty and brokenness. Psalm 119:76–77 says this: *"May your unfailing love be my comfort, according to your promise to your servant. Let your compassion come to me that I may live,..."* The Psalms are filled with the thoughts and feelings you have that are part of being human and living in a broken world. And remember what I wrote earlier: in our pain we *feel* distant from God and others, but it is not the truth. God is near. So in times like these the Scriptures will renew your mind, help you draw near to Him, and remind you of His comfort and compassion. And may you not be overcome with fear.

CHAPTER 11
IF WE ABIDE IN CHRIST, ARE WE TO BE FEARFUL?

John 15:18-21

The previous chapter, which addressed trials in our lives, also raised the question about fear. Often, when we are going through difficult times we are overcome with anxiety and fear. Nothing is more destructive in our lives than worry, fear, and anxiety. These are also the biggest joy and peace robbers. Throughout Scripture—Old and New Testaments—we are told by God and His Son "do not fear" and "do not be afraid." Even when we are facing persecution, as He did when walking this earth, he told his disciples not to fear what would come. We are facing no greater threat from the world or Satan now than they did during the time of Christ and the beginnings of the Church. So it seems important for us to take a closer look at what Scripture has to say about fear.

First, it is important to note, that by speaking the words, "*Do not fear*," God is acknowledging that, from our human perspective, there is cause for fear. However, He always gives a reason, called a promise, as to why we do not need to fear. Let's look at some of these scriptures.

Matthew 14:22–31 says, *"Immediately Jesus made the disciples get into the boat and go on ahead of him to the other side,... During the fourth watch of the night Jesus went out to them, walking on the lake. When the disciples saw him walking on the lake, they were terrified. 'It's a ghost,' they said, and cried in fear. But Jesus immediately said to them: 'Take courage! It is I. Don't be afraid.' 'Lord, if it's you,' Peter replied, 'tell me to come to you on the water.' 'Come,' he said. Then Peter got down out of the boat, walked on the water and came toward Jesus. But when he saw the wind, he was afraid and, beginning to sink, cried out, 'Lord, save me!' Immediately Jesus reached out his hand and caught him. 'You of little faith,' he said, 'why did you doubt?'*

Luke 12:4–11 — *"'I tell you, my friends, do not be afraid of those who kill the body and after that can do no more... Are not five sparrows sold for two pennies? Yet, not one of them is forgotten by God. Indeed, the very hairs of your head are all numbered. Don't be afraid; you are worth more than many sparrows... When you are brought before synagogues, rulers and authorities, do not worry about how you will defend yourselves or what you will say, for the Holy Spirit will teach you at that time what you should say.'"*

Romans 8:15— *"For you did not receive a spirit that makes you a slave again to fear, but you received the Spirit of sonship. And by him we cry, 'Abba, Father,.'"*

2 Timothy 1:7— *"For God did not give us a spirit of timidity/fear, but a spirit of power, of love and of self-discipline."*

I John 4:18— *"There is no fear in love. But perfect love drives out fear,..."*

In every one of the above verses, there was a legitimate reason to fear. Jesus understood the reason and did not criticize them for having the fear. But He gave them, and us, the reason not to fear—His presence, power, and authority over everything in this world. When we study Him in the gospels, do we see Him being afraid of anything or anyone, including the demons? Absolutely not. Through His death and resurrection He conquered death and Satan himself. He has and always will have dominion over them. Colossians 1:13—18 tells us He has control over all. So then, if He is **with us and never leaves us** and He is **in us and we are in Him** why do we live in fear?

This is what Chambers wrote:

Hebrews 13:5–6

My assurance is to be built upon God's assurance to me. God says, "I will never leave you," so that then I "may boldly say, 'The Lord is my helper; I will not fear'" (Hebrews 13:5–6). In other words, I will not be obsessed with apprehension. This does not mean that I will not be tempted to fear, but I will remember God's words of assurance. I will be full of courage, like a child who strives to reach the standard his father has set for him. The faith of many people begins to falter when apprehensions enter their thinking, and they forget the meaning of God's assurance—they forget to take a deep spiritual breath. The only way to remove the fear from our lives is to listen to God's assurance to us.

What are you fearing? Whatever it may be, you are not a coward about it—you are determined to face it, yet you still have a feeling of fear. When it seems that there is nothing and no one to help you, say to yourself, "But 'The Lord is my helper' this very moment, even in my present circumstance." Are you learning to listen to God… Take hold of the Father's assurance, and then say with strong courage, "I will not fear." It does not matter what evil or wrong may be in our way, because "He Himself has said, 'I will never leave you… '"

Human frailty is another thing that gets between God's words of assurance and our own words and thoughts. When we realize how feeble we are in facing difficulties, the difficulties become like giants, we become like grasshoppers, and God seems to be nonexistent. But remember God's assurance to us—*"I will never...forsake you."* Have we learned to sing after hearing God's keynote? Are we continually filled with enough courage to say, "The Lord is my helper," or are we yielding to fear?

We are not fundamentally free; external circumstances are not in our hands, they are in God's hands, the one thing in which we are free is in our personal relationship to God. We are not responsible for the circumstances we are in, but we are responsible for the way we allow those circumstances to affect us; we can either allow them to get on top of us, or we can allow them to transform us into what God wants us to be.[1]

So if we are overcome by fear—the normal, human response—what may be some possible reasons? First reason could be that we don't really believe and acknowledge that He is with/in us. Secondly, we don't really trust Him and trust He has victory and control over everything. We tend to put more trust in the physical, seen things, than the Spiritual, unseen world. If we, like Peter in the Matthew 14:22–31 account, focus on the overwhelming, fearful circumstances, we will be overcome with fear. This is rational and understandable. But if we are told that we need not fear and worry because our Savior is with us, then isn't that enough reason to trust Him and be comforted by His peace?

Now, in writing this, I'm aware of several extenuating factors that make trust more of a challenge for some. If we have experienced abuse, untrustworthy relationships, or betrayal, our brains are wired to be on guard, and we will have difficulty trusting God and others. This Scripture may help if you are experiencing fear at the moment. Romans 8:31, 36–39 says,

> *"If God is for us, who can be against us?... 'For your sake we face death all day long; we are considered as sheep to be slaughtered.' No, in all these things we are more than conquerors through him who loved us. For I am convinced that neither death nor life, neither angels nor demons, neither the present nor the future, nor any powers, neither height nor depth, not anything else in all creation, will be able to separate us from the love of God that is in Christ Jesus our Lord."*

Psalm 46 shares similar thoughts:

> *"God is our refuge and strength, an ever-present help in trouble. Therefore we will not fear, though the earth*

give way and the mountains fall into the heart of the sea, though its waters roar and foam and the mountains quake with their surging... The LORD Almighty is with us; the God of Jacob is our fortress."

There is much upheaval in our world, and I see many becoming angry and fearful in the midst of our current events. Yet, I hear my Father Almighty telling us not to fear. If we are focused on this world, we have every reason to fear. So, the only answer is to keep our eyes on Jesus. Peter was filled with fear and sank into the sea when he took his eyes off Jesus (Matt. 14:30–31). Jesus didn't change Peter's circumstances; He helped him realize that He was the source of courage and peace in the midst of the storm. This is a lesson from which I continually draw and, I pray, you can too.

If you are overcome with fear and anxiety, you may want to try this exercise. In whatever circumstance you find yourself, take a minute to find a comfortable place to sit or lie down, close your eyes, and take a few slow, deep, breaths to relax. Visualize the tension moving out of your head, down into and out of your shoulder and arms, and then moving down through your body and out through your toes. Now, imagine Jesus right there with you. What do you feel? Does seeing Him there with you give you confidence to face your situation? Do you feel His presence? Can you hear His voice, telling you, "I'm with you, My beloved child"? You may want to reach out to hold His hand and tell Him what you fear. Visualize walking with Him through whatever you need to face. Just stay with Him until you feel your anxiety and fear leave and you feel His peace, "the peace that passes all understanding." Slowly open your eyes and remember your experience each time the fear and anxiety comes back into your mind.

This is just one way to help you enter the reality of His presence. Quoting Scripture or simply speaking to Him in open honesty (like the Psalms do), listening to music with a spiritual message, or asking a trusted friend to pray with you are other ways to minimize your anxiety and fear. Our Father and Jesus are just waiting for you to acknowledge His presence and totally trust in Him. I am aware that there is a great deal of uncertainty and turmoil in our world today. And if we depend on ourselves, our government, finances, job, guns, or world peace, we will live in fear and anxiety. Jesus made this promise to His disciples the night before He was crucified: *"Peace I leave with you; my peace I give you. I do not give to you as the world gives. Do not let your hearts be troubled and do not be afraid"* (John 14:27). Remember who you are: children of the Most High, brother and sister to the Son of God, a *"chosen people, a royal priesthood, a holy nation, a people belonging to God, that you may declare the praises of him who called you out of darkness into his wonderful light"* (1 Peter 2:9).

IF WE ABIDE IN CHRIST, ARE WE TO BE FEARFUL?

A writer in Our Daily Bread wrote these words:

Recently as I sat in a circle of leaders from our church, a woman asked a simple question, provoking rich discussion. "What are your hopes for our church?" There were several responses, for our little community has many hopes. But on that night this spilled out of me: "I hope we become more and more the kind of people who learn to resist the anxieties of this world because we believe Jesus is with us and that Jesus is doing something with us."

I've come to believe, more and more, that one of the signs of God's presence with us is our ability to experience Jesus' peace amid a world flooded with fear, restlessness, and suspicion. The ability to receive and live by Jesus' peace is what I hope for me. And this is what I hope for the people in my life.

After Jesus' resurrection,... (He) said, "Peace be with you" and "Why are you frightened?" and "Why are your hearts filled with doubt?" (Luke 24:36,38).

When Jesus arrives, peace or *well-being* arrives as well. Whenever our hearts are riddled with uncertainty or despair, however our heaviest questions press upon us, wherever we are desperate for hope, for light, for the promise that God can make beauty out of ruin—Jesus says, "Peace be with you."[1]

I can only say a hardy, "Amen!!" It is impossible to experience Jesus' peace when we are filled with fear, anxiety, and worry. So, take a minute, be still and draw near to God, and ask Him to search your heart and help you to acknowledge the things you fear. Confess your lack of faith and trust, and ask His forgiveness. Then confess His love, presence, power, and authority in your life, and ask Him to help you to keep your eyes on Him.

CHAPTER 12
"WHAT A PRIVILEGE TO CARRY EVERYTHING TO GOD IN PRAYER"

The words of the hymn—<u>What a Friend We Have In Jesus</u>—jumped out at me when I felt God's leading to write about prayer. One of the verses of this beautiful hymn says,

> What a Friend we have in Jesus,
> All our sins and griefs to bear,
> What a privilege to carry everything to God in prayer.
> Oh what peace we often forfeit,
> Oh what needless pain we bare,
> All because we do not carry everything to God in prayer.[1]

It seems at times that prayer becomes a burden, drudgery, and source of guilt rather than a joy and privilege. We are taught that one way we connect with God's presence is in prayer. Frequently, we make it part of our quiet devotional time, which we struggle to maintain. In the business of our lives, we quickly list our requests in the morning or at night, and feel this is what we should do if we are to be a good Christian. Yet at the same time we hear and even memorize verses such as Philippians 4:4–6:

> *"Rejoice in the Lord always. I will say it again: Rejoice! Let your gentleness be evident to all. The Lord is near. Do not be anxious about anything, but in everything, by prayer and petition, with thanksgiving, present your requests to God. And the peace of God, which transcends all understanding, will guard your hearts and our minds in Christ Jesus".*

Likewise, I Thessalonians 5:16–19 says, *"Rejoice always; pray without ceasing; in everything give thanks; for this is God's will for you in Christ Jesus."* We are painfully aware and feel shame and guilt that we fall far short of these commands. I also lived with these frustrations for many years. I, like probably many of you, would read books on prayer or about people whose lives were centered on prayer. That would help my prayer life for a little while, yet, nothing ever changed. So what do we do about this dilemma?

I have learned that the problem isn't so much that we don't know how to pray or that we don't pray enough, but rather in our misunderstanding of what prayer really is. Like so many verses in Scripture, we interpret them as we read them with our limited understanding. When I studied the correct interpret of prayer, by looking up the

Greek definition, I felt a huge burden fall off my shoulders. I pray it will also encourage those of you who faithfully try to love God with all your heart, mind, soul, and strength.

The Greek meaning of *prayer* is: "to approach, i.e., (lit.) **come near**, visit, **or worship**, assent to; **by the side of, i.e. near to; usually with the place**, time, occasion, or respect, **which is the destination of the relation**; among, at, because of, before, between, **by the house**. In comp., it denotes essentially the same applications, namely, **motion toward, accession to, or nearness as** (emphasis added)," The overwhelming sense of the word is to *draw near* and acknowledging His presence. Talking to God about our needs and concerns is part of drawing near to our heavenly Father, but there is so much more.

If you recall my previous writing and definition of *"abiding"* — remaining in a given state and relation — we are abiding in Christ when we are with and in Him, near Him, alongside Him, and in His household. So if prayer also is a drawing or being near in the same place, then in reality it is more ***a state of being than an act in which I engage***. So, part of our intimate relationship with Him involves sharing, listening, and having deep talks with Him, which is and takes discipline, but it also is just being with Him as we live our daily life. With this new understanding, do you now realize that we are fulfilling the mandates to "pray without ceasing," and that prayer is not only a discipline, it is also part of the *"abiding in Christ."* Why? Because when I am in and with Christ, I *"have the mind of Christ"*

(I Cor. 2:16b), and His attitude toward the Father—one of praise, thanksgiving, and making requests.

Once I fully understood this, joy in the Lord no longer was/is something I have to ask for or force myself to feel; it just is part of being in His presence—the fruit of the Spirit we share. Chambers' shares similar thoughts on I Thessalonians 5:17:

> Our thinking about prayer, whether right or wrong, is based on our own mental conception of it. The correct concept is to think of prayer as the breath in our lungs and the blood from our hearts. Our blood flows and our breathing continues "without ceasing"; we are not even conscious of it, but it never stops. And we are not always conscious of Jesus keeping us in perfect oneness with God, but if we are obeying Him, He always is. Prayer is not an exercise; it is the life of the saint...[2]

An Unexpected Example of Joy in Prayer–January 16th

I woke early to a foggy, cloudy day. My husband was still sleeping, so I had some alone time with God. The forecast predicted high winds later in the day, so I wanted to get my beach walk in early that day. My husband woke and wasn't ready to join me for a walk, so I went on my own. We had had a little tiff prior to my leaving and as

I started my walk, I was focused on the exchange of words between us (to put it another way, I was in a bad mood and certainly far from feeling joy and His presence). It was one of those times of lamenting. There was a slight drizzle, and the beach was more crowded than usual; probably because everyone had the same idea as me. Suddenly, before me there were shafts of sun's rays streaming from the heavy clouds, reaching down to the ocean waves. My response was, "Thank you Father for reminding me that you are present." However, my thoughts quickly returned to the exchange of words earlier; my mood matched the dark clouds threatening up above. As I turned and started back, unexpectedly, the sun broke through the dark clouds, causing the buildings along the beach to glimmer in brilliance. But of even greater beauty were the emerald green colors of the ocean, which up until then had always been just a dull blue grey. The colors were brilliant, which almost took my breath away. I stared in joyous rapture, adoration, and praise at the beauty created by the sun.

    I realized at that moment that this is exactly the effect the presence of the Son of God has in our/my life. If we focus on the gloom and doom of our lives, we miss out on the joy of our salvation. In one quick moment my dark mood was transformed into joy unspeakable. All I could do is keep my eyes on the indescribable beauty before me, drink it in, smile, and exclaim to those I met, "Look at the color of the ocean. Isn't that beautiful?" I couldn't help but feel joy and a desire to share it. Everyone on the beach was in the same situation, but it seemed that I was the only one noticing the gift of beauty given at that moment. It didn't matter to me that others were not responding with the same joy; it didn't dampen my joy, because it was my heavenly Father and Son whose gift I was sharing.

I have found that when I am enveloped in His presence, I often feel this joy, praise, and thankfulness. It is a gratitude that comes from deep within. It is not forced but bubbles up like a spring of water. Aha! Isn't that what Jesus described the Holy Spirit to be to the woman at the well in John 4:4–26? The joy I felt and that we can feel at those moments is His joy, because we are fully present with Him in the unity of the Father, Son, and the indwelling Holy Spirit. This is the essence of prayer, and I don't have to be in deep conversation with God but just be with Him. I can only imagine that is what it must have felt like to Adam and Eve in the Garden of Eden before the fall.

Getting back to my story of walking on the beach, what started out as a time of lamenting and self-pity, turned into an unexpected time of joy, peace, and feeling of Christ's presence. As I continued to focus on Jesus, I could quickly forgive my husband and let go of the offense I had taken. All was right with me and my heavenly and earthly families. This brings me to a very important subject—one I have come to realize, is likely the biggest reason we struggle to experience God's presence, peace, and the joy of His salvation—the topic of forgiveness. I will discuss forgiveness in detail in the next chapter. But before I go there, I want to discuss a related aspect of prayer, namely, the question of whether there can be times when we are unable to take our needs to God in prayer but still abide in Christ?

When I Cannot Carry My Needs to God in Prayer

Recently, my heavenly Father, in His great mercy, opened my eyes to another understanding of prayer. As I have shared earlier, there have been times when I was overwhelmed with grief and pain over difficult circumstances. In those times I would "lament," but at other times I couldn't even pray. Abba used an account recorded in Matthew 9:1–8, when Jesus heals a paralyzed man, to help relieve me of guilt and have a deeper understanding of those times. The man in this story was incapable of drawing near to Jesus, but his friends knew his heart's desire. Filled with faith, *they* carried the paralyzed man to Jesus, who then healed him in an unexpected way. The point is, there are times in our lives that we may be so utterly distressed, that we are as paralyzed, incapable of coming to Jesus, unable to speak or think (pray). These are the times in which we need to let our friends know and ask them to intercede for us—carrying us before Jesus with their faith and trust. Just like Jesus honored the man's friend's act of faith and love and blessed all of them, so too He will bless and honor the intercession of our friends at those times in our lives. It is also important to realize that the paralyzed man was blessed by simply being in Jesus' presence without the ability to do or say anything.

CHAPTER 13
FORGIVENESS, THE KEY TO THE KINGDOM OF HEAVEN, ABIDING JOY, AND PEACE

Matthew 16:13-19; John 20:21-23

One of the commands we are given in Scripture is to "forgive, as we have been forgiven" (Colossians 3:13). The need for forgiveness has existed since the disobedience/sin of Adam and Eve, which caused our separation from our heavenly Father. Reconciliation in the Old Testament was through the detailed sacrificial system; in the New Testament through the sacrifice of Jesus—the "Lamb of God." Many books have been written, many sermons preached, and many counseling sessions have centered on this huge topic of forgiveness. And yet it is an area in which we all struggle, and most likely the reason God wants me to include this topic in this book.

Let's start with the beginning. You may or may not know that, according to Scripture and Christian teaching, we are all born sinners—separated from God, without His indwelling Spirit, and incapable of living a holy life. We cannot attain God's perfection, or dwell in His presence until we admit our sinful state, acknowledge that Jesus is God's Son and the perfect, spotless Lamb who takes away our sin. He accomplished this by becoming sin for us and dying on the cross. When we choose to turn away from our life of sin (repent), and ask God for His forgiveness, we receive total forgiveness and cleansing from all our sins, and the righteousness of Christ is credited to us. We are born anew with His Spirit. We are **"a new Creation"** — reborn to live the life God originally created us to live, like Adam and Eve, a life of loving unity with our Creator.

Here again are Oswald's words:

> If Jesus Christ is going to regenerate me, what is the problem He faces? It is simply this—I have a heredity in which I had no say or decision; I am not holy, nor am I likely to be;... Just as the nature of sin entered into the human race through one man, the Holy Spirit entered into the human race through another Man (Jesus). And redemption mean that I can be delivered from the heredity of sin,..."[1] "Sin is a fundamental relationship—it is not wrong *doing*, but wrong *being*—it is deliberate and determined independence from God. The first thing Jesus Christ confronted in people was the heredity of sin,... The revealed truth of the Bible is not that Jesus Christ took on Himself our fleshly sins, but that He took on Himself the heredity

of sin that no man can even touch. God made His own Son "to be sin" that He might make the sinner into a saint... Jesus Christ reconciled the human race, putting it back to where God designed it to be. And now anyone can experience that reconciliation, being brought into oneness with God, on the basis of what our Lord had done on the cross.[2]

The very foundation of our relationship with our heavenly Father and His Son, Jesus, is built on the act of forgiveness, a power that intellectually is neither easily explained nor understood and even harder to live out. I can't count all the verses that speak of forgiveness; they include the command that we are to forgive others as Christ has forgiven us. But the Scripture that my Father has used to help me understand the importance of forgiveness and that I want to use as the focus in this book, is in Matthew 16:13–19.

"When Jesus came to the region of Caesarea Philippi, he asked his disciples, 'Who do people say the Son of Man is?' They replied, 'Some say John the Baptist; others say Elijah; and still others, Jeremiah or one of the prophets.' 'But what about you?' he asked. 'Who do you say I am?' Simon Peter answered, 'You are the Christ, the Son of the living God.' Jesus replied, 'Blessed are you, Simon son of Jonah, for this was not

> *revealed to you by man, but by my Father in heaven. And I tell you that you are Peter, and on this rock I will build my church, **and the gates of Hades will not overcome it. I will give you the keys of the kingdom of heaven; whatever you bind on earth will be bound in heaven, and whatever you loose on earth will be loosed in heaven** (emphasis added).*"

This Scripture's cross-references is John 20:22–23, which says, "'*Peace be with you. As the Father has sent me, I am sending you.' And with that he breathed on them and said, 'Receive the Holy Spirit. **If you forgive anyone his sins, they are forgiven; if you do not forgive them, they are not forgiven*** (emphasis added).'"

It is critical that we interpret Scripture in its full context. Jesus responds to Peter's confession (Matt. 16) with two statements: first, only My Father in Heaven gave you this revelation; second, the church will be built on the foundation of this truth. Third, the very power of hell will not overcome it. The only way into God's kingdom is through acceptance and acknowledgment that Jesus is the Son of God, the promised Messiah. There is no other "way, truth, and life" (John 14:6). Jesus then follows those statements in the Matthew 16 account by saying that He will give "*the keys of the kingdom of heaven*" to those (His disciples) who have made this confession of faith. Those keys are none other than the act of forgiveness. The key is a symbolic image, which He accurately used to describe a process.

To better understand Jesus' use of this symbol and imagery, we need to go to the Greek definition of several words. ***Key***—"a key (as shutting or lock to close)." ***Bind/bound*)**—"be in bonds, knit, beloved, to be (binding oneself)." ***Loose***—"to loosen, break (up), destroy, dissolve, put off." Bear with me as I carefully unlock (no pun intended) these truths. First, Jesus is saying, that the key (ability to lock or unlock the door to His kingdom) is given to those who believe that He is the Messiah, the Son of God, and this key is receiving and giving—forgiveness/loosing. So, the first blessing, after our confession of faith, is the forgiveness of all our sins (past, present, and even future).

Second, this key is also the (only) power to set us free from the bonds of Satan and his kingdom by shutting and locking him out. The image of the key is like that of a key to our new home (the kingdom of Heaven), and the same key is used to lock out the enemy, who wants to steel and destroy. We are given the authority and power, by and through Christ, to use it or not—to be bound to and be the *beloved* of the Kingdom of God or the kingdom of Satan/the world.

Third, those who have received the key (Jesus' disciples) also have been given the command (and authority) to lock the door against the influences of the enemy, by forgiving—"*loosing, breaking, destroying, dissolving, putting off*" sin and the power of Satan in others. This means choosing to forgive those who have sinned against us. By choosing this act (to use the key) we are accomplishing several, powerful, spiritual battles: (1) we keep the door to our lives locked against the enemy's influences; (2) we loose (release) the one who has sinned against us to be unbound from the enemy, and commit them into God's hands for judgment (or mercy) as He in His infinite wisdom determines; (3) we are unbound, loosened from the effects of the one who has sinned against us; (4) it sets us free from, or keeps us from developing the root of bitterness, which will poison our lives. *We are set free to be protected and have all the blessings, security, and joy of our new home in the kingdom of Heaven.* Once again, Jesus is our best example of this truth as recorded in 1 Peter 2:21–23: "

> *"To this you were called, because Christ suffered for you, leaving you an example, that you should follow in his steps. He committed no sin, and no deceit was found in his mouth. When they hurled their insults at him, he did not retaliate; when he suffered, he made no threats. Instead, he entrusted himself to him who judges justly."*

We all struggle to forgive. The world, the flesh, and the devil are using all their forces to keep us out of the Kingdom of Heaven, to deprive us from the blessing of Christ, and to keep our lives in disarray, despair, bent on destruction. To put it bluntly, to have us living in hell. Usually, when we have been wounded, all our focus is on the person who has wounded us. We are not aware that the battle is actually a spiritual one, not simply a problem with humanity. This is how Ephesians 6:1, 2 describes this battle:

> *"Finally, be strong in the Lord and in his mighty power. Put on the full armor of God so that you can take your stand against the devil's schemes. For our struggle is not against flesh and blood, but against the rulers, against the authorities, against the powers of this dark world and against the spiritual forces of evil in the heavenly realms."*

It takes humility to admit our sin. This state of humility is one of the traits of Christ Himself, which we need to learn, or rather said, surrender to, since it is totally contrary to our old fleshly nature. The nature of the world, the flesh, and the devil is pride. Usually, we have difficulty in forgiving others because we think we are better than them (stubborn pride) and that they don't deserve our or God's mercy and blessing. Because we have been unjustly treated we believe we have the right to hurt them back, punish them, and hold onto our anger. Satan, who is called the deceiver and destroyer, will cause us to believe that we don't need to receive or give forgiveness and that there is power, control, and safety in holding onto our anger and bitterness. We want to stand on *our right* to be treated justly. But sadly, these lies are the power of Satan, which keep us in chains. Listen to the words in James 4:1–10.

> *"He jealously desires the Spirit which He has made to dwell in us"… Therefore it says, "God is opposed to the proud, but gives grace to the humble." Submit, therefore to God. Resist the devil and he will flee from you. Draw near to God and He will draw near to you. Cleanse your hands, you sinners; and purify your hearts, you double-minded… Humble yourselves in the presence of the Lord, and He will exalt you…"*

Satan's power over us is in pride and unforgiveness. And that is his goal, for it renders us as Christians and the church ineffective. Jesus made it very clear to His disciples that the effectiveness of our witness is through unity of the body and the love we show to one another. I Peter 3:8–9 says this: *"Finally, all of you, live in harmony with one another; be sympathetic, love as brothers, be compassionate and humble. Do not repay evil with evil or insult with insult, but with blessing, because to this you were called so that you may inherit a blessing."* It is apparent in these verses that we can only live the abiding life in Christ through the grace and forgiveness of sin in our own lives and those of others. The most difficult, yet most powerful and blessed act is the act of forgiveness. To sum it up, it is only in forgiveness that Satan will be rendered powerless. And it is only through forgiveness that the unity, the bond of oneness, will be kept strong with Him and others.

These are just a few of a multitude of Scriptures, which talk about forgiveness. Peter once asked Jesus this question: *"'Lord, how many times shall I forgive my brother when he sins against me? Up to seven times?' Jesus answered, 'I tell you, not seven times, but seventy-seven times (Matt. 18:21–22).'"* This account was followed by a stern warning, in the form of a parable, of the high cost of unforgiveness. I strongly urge you to also read this parable in Matthew 18:21–35, "Jesus tells *the Parable of the Unforgiving Debtor.*"

Since forgiveness is the only bases for true healing and restoration of relationships, can you understand more clearly the incredible gift and responsibility we have been given by Christ? This is why it is given as a command instead of a suggestion or recommendation. If we neglect this important command it is easy to see why this world and our lives are filled with so much brokenness, anger, hatred, and emotional sickness. Sadly, even within the church, which is called *"the body of Christ,"* this same brokenness exists. Divorce and division are as prevalent in the church as in the secular world. I believe it is because we have overlooked and neglected this powerful gift (key) availed to us through and in Christ. Instead, we go about justifying our sins and weakness, judging others for theirs, building walls of defense, and trying to feel in control with our own power and ego. Then we wonder: where is God; why don't we have peace; why isn't my life changing to be more like Christ; why don't we have more joy in our lives? If we desire to live in the freedom, peace, wholeness, and joy of the Kingdom of God (our new home), then the only choice for us is to choose to use the key and ask and give forgiveness.

Some accounts in the Bible, which demonstrate the wonderful blessings of forgiveness, are found in Luke 7:36–50: the women who lived a sinful life and Luke 15:11–31: the Parable of the Lost Son. In both, the humility of acknowledging the sin and coming to Jesus or the Father gained them the powerful, spiritual act of forgiveness and restoration. I believe, in the depth of our hearts, this is what all of us seek and hunger for. Can you relate to a time when you experienced real forgiveness for a sin, and received the peace, love, and joy that resulted in an immediate deep healing of your soul? I can.

Before I close this chapter on forgiveness, I think it is important to, briefly, clear up some frequent misunderstandings about forgiveness—what it is and what it is not.

Forgiveness–What it is and What it is Not

1) "Forgiveness is not forgetting. When God says that He will 'not remember your sins' (Isaiah 43:25), He is saying that He will not use the past against us"; He will not keep rehearsing and re-memorizing our sin.

2) "Forgiveness is a choice, a decision of the will"; it is not based on feelings. "Do not wait for the other person to ask for your forgiveness."
3) "Forgiveness is agreeing to live with the consequences of another person's sin." We all suffer the consequences of sin, including our own, because we live in a broken world.
4) "Forgive from your heart," which means allowing yourself to be honest with yourself, God, and the other person (if possible) about the pain the sin has caused. He desires truth in the innermost part.
5) "Forgiveness is choosing not to hold someone's sin against him or her any longer." You choose to let go (loose) them of your right to pay back evil for evil, and commit them and yourself into God's hand for judgment. I Peter 2:23 says this: *"When they hurled their insults at him, he did not retaliate; when he suffered, he made no threats. Instead, he entrusted himself to him who judges justly."*
6) "Don't wait until you feel like forgiving." In time God will heal the damaged emotions.[3]

You may want to use this model of a prayer: "Lord Jesus, I choose to forgive (name of the person) for (what he/she did or failed to do), because it made me feel (share the painful feelings). I choose not to hold on to my resentment. I relinquish my right to seek revenge and ask You to heal my damaged emotions. Thank You for setting me free from the bondage of my bitterness. I now ask You to bless those who have hurt me. In Jesus' name I pray. Amen."[4]

If you continue to struggle and feel captive to the negative emotions connected to old experiences, it may be helpful to see a Christian counselor to walk with you, and support you through your pain and grief, and forgiveness process.

CHAPTER 14
I JUST WANT TO BE WHERE YOU ARE

As I come to a close, I asked my Father what final thoughts He would like to share. The words from this song came to mind.

> I just want to be where you are;
> Dwelling daily in your presence.
> I don't want to worship from afar;
> Draw me near to where you are.
>
> I just want to be where you are;
> In your dwelling place forever.
> Take to the place where you are;
> I just want to be with you.
>
> In your presence,
> That's where I always want to be.
> Feasting at your table;
> Surrounded by your glory.
>
> I just want to be where you are;
> (repeat)[1]

The words of this beautiful song sum up the main thoughts of the abiding life in Christ and the joy of our salvation. It is my prayer, that as you read this book you have heard the voice and heart of the Father and Jesus, His beloved Son.

I hope you have walked with me as I shared some of my life-changing experiences, in which I have heard the Father's teaching and am trying to walk it out to this day. My prayer has been that you have also heard Jesus calling you to saying, *"Come to Me."* If you are weary and troubled with burdens, may you embrace His love, protection, and grace as you come to fully live in the *household* He has given you, here and now.

I trust Jesus' Spirit has opened the eyes of your understanding to know and see the many ways you may have been deprived of the joy of His presence, and the reasons you may feel distant from your heavenly Father. As we learned from Jesus, He is more than *"the Way, the Truth, and the Life"* unto salvation, [so] may we continually *"fix our eyes on Jesus, the author and perfecter of our faith"* (Hebrews 12:2). I would like to suggest, that if you feel overwhelmed with all the information in this book, you may want to ask Jesus to show you which truth (application) He wants you to begin walking out in your life. As we have read, He is the Way, and He will direct your path according to the knowledge He has of your life and struggles. We usually don't do well if we start too many new behaviors at one time. Remember, He is the one who is the righteousness of God and enables you to live a life pleasing to the Father. One of the first Scriptures I memorized and encouraged me was Philippians 2:13: *"For it is God who works in you to will and to act according to his good purpose."* May this truth also encourage you in your desire and commitment to walk out your salvation.

You may have noticed that I have given just a few "how to" suggestions. This is very intentional, since I don't want you to be Maria's disciple, but Jesus' disciple. My (and I believe Jesus') heart's desire is for you to start hearing His voice and learning to apply His truth to your personal situations. As I stated in one of my earlier chapters, we tend to rely too often on "self-help" books instead of turning to *"the Counselor."* I believe God's purpose of this book is to encourage you to go to **the Author** of the greatest book ever written—the Bible—rather than just relying on others for direction, wisdom, and suggestions on how to live the life of Christ. We all can be used to teach and learn, but lessons learned directly from the Master/Teacher, tend to have the deepest and long-lasting impact on our lives. The following quote is a word of wisdom from Oswald: "It is impossible to read too much, but always keep before you why you read. Remember that 'the need to receive, recognize, and rely on the Holy Spirit' is before all else."[2]

As we have drawn close to Jesus and your mind has been renewed by some of His teaching, I pray you have come to know the One who is the source of all love, joy, peace, patience, kindness, goodness, faithfulness, and self-control. May you find new joy as you learn to stop striving to *be like Him by imitating Him*, and learn to surrender (*integrate*) His righteousness.

In this busy world, I hope you occasionally choose the most needed thing—sitting at Jesus feet—or walking with Him as the Word who is still teaching and opening our eyes. May your heart burn with joy and excitement as you hear Him explain Scripture to you—His beloved disciple and friend. Remember, He still desires to sow the seed of His word into your heart. Will you be the fertile soil to receive it and bear much fruit? As you learn to live the abiding life, may the gifts of the Spirit empower your life of service to minister and build up the body of Christ, the church, and be a witness of Christ's love.

As long as we live on this earth we will have pain and sorrow. I hope you are in process of realizing that we are not spared this pain just because we are Christians. But, may you remember God's promises that we need not fear because He is always with us and in us. He bears the sorrow with us, if we turn and trust Him to carry it. Most of all, I pray you have begun to realize that we do not need to live in fear of any circumstance we face. Our loving heavenly Father has been, and always will be, in total control. Not a sparrow will fall without His awareness.

Walking out the truths of chapter 13—forgiveness—most likely, is going to be the greatest challenge—one we will only be able to do with and in Christ. Forgiveness begins with our life in Christ and is only possible through Christ. My pastor once made this statement: "Because we cannot change (or undo) the past, all we can (and are commanded to) do is forgive it."[3] In Christ we have been given the greatest gift of love and peace—the key of forgiveness. As we learned,

ABIDING

it is the power we have been given to set us free from the kingdom of Satan, to stay protected within the Kingdom of God, and to release (loose) from our past and those who have injured us. This key has been given to us by a Savior who has welcomed us—His beloved—into His home—a home filled with unconditional love, peace, abundant fruit, rest from our labor, and joy unspeakable; the joy of salvation in His eternal presence.

I will close with these verses from Acts 17:24-28:

> *"The God who made the world and everything in it is the Lord of heaven and earth and does not live in temples built by hands. And he is not served by human hands, as if he needed anything, because he himself gives all men life and breath and everything else. From one man he made every nation of men, that they should inhabit the whole earth; and he determined the times set for them and the exact places where they should live. God did this so that men would seek him and perhaps reach out for him and find him, though he is not far from each one of us. For in him we live and move and have our being… 'We are his offspring.'"*

Amen

NOTES

All definitions given from the Hebrew and Greek language are quoted from The New Strong's Exhaustive Concordance of the Bible – Thomas Nelson Publishers, Nashville, Camden, Kansas City

All English definitions are taken from The American Heritage Dictionary of The English Language – 3rd Edition, 1992 by Houghton Mifflin Company, Boston, New York, London

The Complete Works of Oswald Chambers, C 2000 by Oswald Chambers Publications Association, Limited

My Utmost For His Highest – The Golden Book of Oswald Chambers, Discovery House Publishers, RBC Ministries, Grand Rapids, Nashville, Tennessee 37214

Our Daily Bread – Our Daily Bread Ministries, Grand Rapids, Michigan

Our Daily Journey–Our Daily Bread Ministries, Grand Rapids, Michigan

Bread for the Journey: A Daybook of Wisdom and Faith by Henri Nouwen – Harper San Francisco, 1997,

Living At HIS Place by Jim May – Fifth Edition by Building on the Rock, Inc, Lakewood, CO 80227

Black Ice When Life Changes in a Second by Jim May – Outskirtspress, Denver, Colorado

The Steps To Freedom in Christ by Neil T. Anderson – 2004, Published by Bethany House Publishers, Bloomington, Minnesota 55438

Pastor Chris Shearer – Pastor of River Tree Community Church, Wyoming, Michigan

Introduction
- [1] My Utmost For His Highest – The Golden Book of Oswald Chambers

Chapter 2
- [1] Babbie Mason

Chapter 3
- [1] January 7–My Utmost For His Highest – The Golden Book of Oswald Chambers

Chapter 4
- [1] February 10–My Utmost For His Highest

NOTES

[2] – Wisdom and Faith by Henri Nouwen

[3] – August 19–My Utmost For His Highest – The Golden Book of Oswald Chambers

[4] – April 3–My Utmost For His Highest – The Golden Book of Oswald Chambers

[5] – Matt Crocker, Joel Houston, Salomon Ligtheim—Hillsong United; Zion,Sept. 2013

Chapter 5

[1] – The Psychology of Redemption, 1066L–The Complete Works of Oswald Chambers

[2] – January 13–My Utmost For His Highest – The Golden Book of Oswald Chambers

[3] – Page 27–Black Ice When Life Changes in a Second by Jim May

[4] –Approved Unto God, 11 L–The Complete Works of Oswald Chambers

Chapter 6

[1] – Page 27–Living At HIS Place by Jim May

[2] – April 9–My Utmost For His Highest – The Golden Book of Oswald Chambers

[3] – April 8–My Utmost For His Highest – The Golden Book of Oswald Chambers

[4] – June 11–My Utmost For His Highest – The Golden Book of Oswald Chambers

ABIDING

[5] – June 12–My Utmost For His Highest – The Golden Book of Oswald Chambers

[6] – March 19, 761L–My Utmost For His Highest

[7] – Page 117–Living At HIS Place by Jim May

Chapter 7

[1] – March 21–My Utmost For His Highest – The Golden Book of Oswald Chambers

[2] – The American Heritage Dictionary of The English Language

[3] – The American Heritage Dictionary of The English Language

[4] – July 23–My Utmost For His Highest – The Golden Book of Oswald Chambers

Chapter 8

[1] – January 28–My Utmost For His Highest

[2] – Our Brilliant Heritage, 946R–The Complete Works of Oswald Chambers

Chapter 9

[1] – The American Heritage Dictionary of The English Language

[2] – Strong's Concordance Helps Word-studies

Chapter 10

[1] – Page 164–Living At HIS Place by Jim May

[2] – April 3, 2016 by Sheridan Voysey–Our Daily Journey

NOTES

[3] – June 5, 2016 by Peter Chin–Our Daily Journey

[4] – March 7–My Utmost For His Highest

[5] – January 20, 2016 by Dave Branon – Our Daily Bread

Chapter 11

[1] – June 5–My Utmost For His Highest

[2] Conformed to His Image, 354L–The Complete Works of Oswald Chambers

[3] – Page 3 by Winn Collier–Our Daily Bread

Chapter 12

[1] – Joseph M. Scriven—Hymns for the Family of God

[2] –My Utmost For His Highest

Chapter 13

[1] – October 6–My Utmost For His Highest

[2] – October 7–My Utmost For His Highest

[3] – The Steps to Freedom in Christ by Neil T. Anderson

[4] –The Steps to Freedom in Christ by Neil T. Anderson

Chapter 14

[1] – Don Moen

[2] Approved Unto God, 11 L–The Complete Works of Oswald Chambers

[3] –Pastor Chris Shearer